Writing Papers
in
Psychology

Writing Papers
in
Psychology

A Student Guide

Ralph L. Rosnow
Temple University

Mimi Rosnow

Wadsworth Publishing Company
Belmont, California
A Division of Wadsworth, Inc.

Psychology Editor: Kenneth King
Editorial Assistant: Linda Cazanov
Production Editor: Sandra Craig
Print Buyer: Ruth Cole
Cover and Text Designer: Paula Shuhert
Copy Editor: Pat Tompkins
Compositor: Graphic Typesetting Service
Signing Representative: Joyce Larcom

Printed in the United States of America

3 4 5 6 7 8 9 10—90 89 88 87

ISBN 0-534-06780-8

Library of Congress Cataloging-in-Publication Data

Rosnow, Ralph L.
  Writing papers in psychology.

  Includes index.
  1. Psychology--Authorship. 2. Report writing.
I. Rosnow, Mimi, 1938–   . II. Title.
BF76.7.R67 1986   808'.06615   86–5489
ISBN 0–534–06780–8

To the partnership that brought this book about

Ralph L. Rosnow, Ph.D.
is Thaddeus Bolton Professor of Psychology and
Director of the Social Psychology Division at Temple University.

Mimi Rosnow
is a free-lance copy editor with a degree in English
from Wheaton College, Norton, Massachusetts.

Contents

5

Writing and Revising 27

6

Layout and Typing 36

A

Sample Term Paper 45

B

Sample Research Report 55

Preface

Whether or not one subscribes to the notion that writing is an "unnatural act" (as some writers have claimed with tongue in cheek), it is basic to the educational process. In an age where television pictures and the spoken word seem to prevail, the written word has a unique, indeed almost old-fashioned power to compel, persuade, convince—that is, to communicate ideas. We hope this manual will help make the process of communicating ideas in the research report and term paper a learning experience that will provide the student with new appreciation of the rigors and rewards of well-written papers. We wish to leave the student with a profound sense of satisfaction and joy that we associate with effective written communication.

The plan of the manual (shown in the flowchart on the next page) coincides with the steps involved in developing the research report and the term paper. We contrast the two forms and then explain how a student proceeds from choosing a subject, using the library, structuring the paper, and writing and polishing it to typing the final draft. Except for Chapters 3 and 4, the information presented is applicable to both the term paper and the research report, as well as to papers required in a variety of subjects.

We do not discuss the technical requirements of constructing hypotheses, gathering data, and analyzing the research findings; we assume that the student assigned to write a research report is being taught these skills with the aid of a general methods text. Our personal preference in such texts is (not surprisingly) *Essentials of Behavioral Research: Methods and Data Analysis* for advanced students and *Understanding Behavioral Science: Research Methods for Research Consumers* for beginning students (both by R. Rosenthal and R. L. Rosnow and published by McGraw-Hill). Although Chapter 5 has style tips, we assume that the student has mastered essential writing techniques; if not, or if basic skills need polishing, the student can choose from a wide range of composition guides. We did not want to burden students with a manual so technical and detailed that it could serve as the basic text in a writing course.

Embark on the project
(Chapter 1)

↓

Begin a literature search
(Chapter 2)

If writing a term paper,	If writing a research report,
develop an outline	structure the content
(Chapter 3)	(Chapter 4)

Write and polish the paper
(Chapter 5)

↓

Type the final draft
(Chapter 6)

For graduate students and others who desire a comprehensive guide to preparing a research article or review for publication in a journal using the APA format, there is no substitute for the *Publication Manual of the American Psychological Association*. For tables, figures, reference citations, nonsexist language, and certain other practical considerations, we follow the style recommended by the APA manual (third edition). However, we are not sticklers for professional guidelines for student papers, and we recommend simple formats for writing the research report and term paper in psychology and education. The sample papers in Appendixes A and B were prepared in this modified style. For example, the research report includes a section for raw data, statistical computations, and questionnaires developed by the student specifically for the project.

We found the APA manual, information sheets provided by Temple University's Paley Library, and the following texts invaluable in reminding us of technical points we might have otherwise forgotten to mention in this student guide: R. Barrass's *Scientists Must Write* (Wiley, 1978); R. W. Bly and G. Blake's *Technical Writing: Structure, Standard, and Style* (McGraw-Hill, 1982); D. E. Fear's *Technical Writing* (Random House, 1973); H. R. Fowler's *The Little, Brown Handbook* (Little, Brown, 1983); K. W. Houp and T. E. Pearsall's *Reporting Technical Information* (Macmillan, 1984). M. H. Markel's *Technical Writing: Situations and Strategies* (St. Martin's Press, 1984); D.J.D. Mulkerne and D.J.D. Mulkerne, Jr.'s *The Term Paper* (Anchor Press/Doubleday, 1983); L. A. Olsen and T. N. Huchin's *Principles of Communication for Science and Technology* (McGraw-Hill, 1957); K. L. Turabian's *A Manual for Writers of Term Papers, Theses and Dissertations* (University of Chicago Press, 1955); and J. E. Warriner's *Handbook of English* (Harcourt, Brace, 1951).

We thank Maria Di Medio and John Yost for permission to edit their papers and to include the edited versions in this manual. We are indebted to John B. Best, Eastern Illinois University; James W. Kalat, North Carolina State University; Allan Kimmel, Moravian College; Mary Lu Rosenthal, Analysis and Computer

Systems; Robert Rosenthal, Harvard University; and Gordon W. Russell, University of Lethbridge, for commenting on an earlier draft of the manuscript and to many psychology and education professors at Temple University and the University of Pennsylvania for suggesting items for our list of commonly misspelled words, especially to Charles Thomas, University of Pennsylvania. We thank Mary Gergen for testing the prepublication manuscript in her Psychology of Gender class at Pennsylvania State University and Sam Fung, John Govern, and Maria Di Medio for trying out portions of the manuscript in their tutorial sections of Psych 274 at Temple University. Ralph Rosnow wishes to acknowledge the support that he has received from Temple University in the form of the Bolton Professorship.

R. L. R.

M. R.

1

Getting Started

The term paper and the research report are distinctly different forms that share certain similarities: both have a relatively simple format; both are written for a specific reader, the instructor; and both require that the project be paced so that you complete the assignment on schedule and it represents your best work. This chapter focuses on the rudiments of getting started on either assignment.

Know Your Objective

Before you do anything else, make sure you understand the assignment. Do not hesitate to ask the instructor if you are not sure what is expected of you. You can talk with other students to get their impressions, but it is always a good idea to check with the instructor to make certain that you are on the right track. One student in every class seems to go off on a tangent and then suffers the consequences of being penalized with a low grade—do not let that student be you. Here is a checklist of some preliminary questions to ask yourself:

- What is the general subject of the assignment?
- Within this subject, do you choose the topic, or has it been assigned by the instructor?
- Has the length of the paper been specified?
- Are progress reports required?
- When is the final report due?

A sense of the differences between the term paper and the research report will help you direct your efforts toward a particular end product. There are three major differences between the two forms. First, a literature search will usually form the core of the term paper, whereas data will form the core of the research report and the literature search will involve only a few key studies that serve as a theoretical starting point. Second, the structure of the term paper, although somewhat formal, is more flexible than that of the research report, which has a standardized structure.

Third, the objective of the term paper is to put issues and ideas into a context of a particular thesis, whereas the objective of the research report is to describe your research findings to others.

Types of Term Papers and Research Reports

To get a better idea of the differences between the research report and the term paper, examine the samples at the back of this manual. The somewhat abbreviated term paper in Appendix A is an example of one of three major types, known as an **expository term paper**. The purpose of the expository term paper is to inform the reader on a specific subject—in this case, treatments for anorexia nervosa. Other expository assignments might be to write a term paper on the concept of IQ or on the phenomenon of higher-order learning or on feeding and the hunger drive. The second type is the **argumentative term paper**, which aims to persuade the reader. Thus you might write a term paper arguing the cost-effectiveness of behavior therapy in comparison to some other current psychotherapeutic approach or a term paper that argues for the validity of cognitive dissonance theory in social psychology. Note that the sample term paper, though not specifically an argumentative paper, does conclude with an opinion about the general therapeutic approach that seems to be more effective. The third type is the **descriptive term paper**, which evokes a situation or event by focusing on distinguishing details. Examples of this type might include a case study involving some personal experience or a narrative interpretation of a particular event. If your assignment is to write a term paper, make sure you know which of these three types—expository, argumentative, or descriptive—the instructor expects.

There are also three major types of research approaches and reports: descriptive, relational, and experimental. A **descriptive research report** carefully maps out its subject; it expresses how things are. For example, you might report the observations you made of freshmen students thrown together for the first time as roommates in a dormitory. A **relational research report** explores the way in which events are related or the way behavior is correlated with another variable. You might report, for example, how college students behave differently toward one another over time. Appendix B, the sample research paper of student John Yost, is a relational research report. He considers the difference in people's confidence in rumors and how that difference relates to the subject's transmission of rumors. Thus reports of relational research describe relationships. The third approach is the **experimental research report**, which details what happens when something of interest to the experimenter is introduced into the situation. For example, you might report a study of how social behavior in rats is affected when the experimenter manipulates the animals' reinforcement schedule. The experimental research report is designed to tell how things become the way they are, or what causes what. Once you have chosen a suitable topic and developed your research hypothesis, focus on the type of report most appropriate to the situation as you wish to study it. Within these three major categories are many specific methods and procedures that you will find detailed in a number of textbooks.

Scheduling Time

Once you are certain that you know what is expected of you, develop a schedule that you feel is realistic. Do not set deadlines that you know you cannot meet. You know your own energy level, so pick realistic dates by which you can reasonably expect to complete each major part of your assignment. Write the dates on your calendar or, better still, post them over your desk as a daily reminder.

Look at the samples in Appendixes A and B, and you see that writing a term paper will require a different time schedule than writing a research report. Writing a term paper usually requires spending a lot of time in the library accumulating source materials. Unless you are assigned more than one paper in a course, most term papers are ten to twenty pages long. Maria Di Medio's paper in Appendix A illustrates the recommended format of an expository term paper, not its recommended length. If you are assigned a term paper, be sure to leave ample time for the following major tasks:

- Completion of outline of term paper
- Completion of library work
- Completion of first draft of term paper
- Completion of revised draft(s) of term paper
- Completion of final draft of term paper

The sample research report in Appendix B is about the usual length of an undergraduate research report, though the results section can vary considerably depending on the data analyses required. Writing such a paper typically requires much less time spent in the library but a lot of time working with your data. If you are assigned a research report, be sure to set aside ample time for these major tasks:

- Completion of proposal for research
- Completion of data collection
- Completion of data analysis
- Completion of first draft of research report
- Completion of revised draft(s) of research report
- Completion of final draft of research report

By scheduling your time, you will not be rushed with imaginary deadlines or surprised as the real deadline approaches. Get started right away—do not procrastinate. Good writing and organizing and revising your writing will take time. Library research does not always go smoothly; a book or journal article you need might be unavailable. Data collection and analysis can also run into snags; the research subjects might not cooperate or the computer might be down. If you get started early, you will have time to write to authors for unpublished or follow-up manuscripts if you think you need them. (Many students often are surprised to learn that they can actually write to an author of a research study and thereby learn of the author's most recent work.)

Instructors have heard all the excuses for a late or badly done paper, so do not expect much sympathy if you miss the final deadline. Note that both schedules of tasks allow time between the first and final draft to distance yourself from your writing. That way you can return to your project with a fresh perspective as you polish the first draft and check for errors in logic, flow, spelling, punctuation, grammar, and typing.

Choosing a Topic

Another difference between the term paper and the research report will quickly become evident even as you begin to think about getting started on your assignment. The topic for the research report will be a given; your hypothesis, data collection, and results will point in a direction so specific that the research report evolves, topic and all, as the final step in a well-regulated procedure. In contrast, the selection of a suitable topic for a term paper is an integral part of learning because you are usually free to explore experiences, observations, and ideas to help you focus on specific topics that will sustain your curiosity and interest as work on the paper progresses.

In considering a suitable topic, beware of a few pitfalls to avoid. Here are some "dos" and "don'ts" that might might make your life easier as you start choosing a topic:

- Be enthusiastic and strive for a positive attitude.
- Use the indexes and tables of contents of standard textbooks as well as class notes for initial leads or ideas you would like to explore more fully.
- Choose a topic that piques your curiosity.
- Make sure your topic can be covered in the available time and the assigned number of pages.
- Don't be afraid to ask your instructor for suggestions.
- Don't choose a topic that you know other students have chosen. You will be competing with them for access to the library's source materials.

Narrowing the Topic

Choosing too broad or too narrow a topic for a term paper or research report will surely add difficulties and will also mean an unsatisfactory result. A term paper topic that is too broad, for example, "Freud's Life and Times," would try to cover too much material within the term paper's limited framework. A specific aspect of Freud's life and times would prove a more appropriately narrowed focus for treatment in a term paper. However, in narrowing the topic, do not limit your discussion to facts that are already well known. Be sure that your topic is not so narrow that reference materials will not be readily available. Be guided by your instructor's advice. If you approach the instructor with several concrete ideas for projects, he or she is usually glad to help tailor those ideas so that student, topic, and project format are compatible.

Here are some examples of how you might begin to narrow the topic of a term paper about Sigmund Freud by a specific working title. (You can always change the title later, once you have finished your library search and have a better sense of the topic.)

Unlimited topic

"Life and Times of Sigmund Freud"

Slightly limited topic

"Psychological Theories of Sigmund Freud"

Limited to twenty-page paper

"Freud's Theory of Personality Applied to Mental Health"

Limited to ten-page paper

"Freud's Theory of Infantile Sexuality"

Too limited

"Freud's Pets"

Here is another example of limiting the topic. This assignment is a research project, and the student must choose a topic in the area of communication to study:

Unlimited topic

"Who Gossips and Why?"

Slightly limited topic

"When Do People Gossip?"

Adequately limited topic

"Content Analysis of Selected Gossip Columns over a Specified Period"

Know Your Audience and Topic

All professional writers know they are writing for a particular audience. This knowledge helps them determine the tone and style of their work. Think of a journalist's report of a house fire and contrast it with a short story describing the same event. Knowing your audience is no less important when the writer is a college student and the project is a term paper or a research report. The audience is your instructor, whose standards and expectations will probably be communicated to you when the project is assigned. Should you have any doubt about the instructor's expectations, find out what they are before you set to work.

Let us assume that you know your audience—your instructor. Now you must try to cultivate more than just a superficial understanding of your subject. The more you read about it and discuss your ideas with friends, the more you will begin to develop an intuitive understanding of the topic. Many writers find it helpful to keep 3 x 5-inch index cards in their pockets to jot down relevant ideas that suddenly occur to them. This is a good way to keep your subject squarely in your mind.

You must comprehend your source material, so equip yourself with a good desk dictionary and turn to it routinely whenever you come across an unfamiliar word. While you are in the market for a dictionary, you might also buy a thesaurus. It can be useful as an index of terms in information retrieval, besides being a treasury of synonyms and antonyms when you write.

2

Using the Library

If you have never set foot in your college library, now is the time to familiarize yourself with its many resources. An afternoon spent perusing the variety of reference materials available (periodicals, standard texts, and abstracts, for example) should be enough to focus your interest on an appropriately specific topic. This chapter will guide you in collecting information from the books and articles available on your particular topic.

Plan of the Library

Begin to familiarize yourself with the library's floor plan if you are not sure where its major sections are located. You might ask at the information desk whether there is a fact sheet available that specifies the ground rules for using the library. If none is available, you can write your own fact sheet as you proceed on an orientation tour of the building. It is inconvenient to return to the information desk every time you have a question, so be aware of other places you can turn to for assistance. Library staff members (often called information librarians today) are also usually available at the reference desk and the catalog desk. Each of these provides specialized help in orienting library users to the resources at hand.

Here is a quick summary of what you can expect to find at each of these three locations:

- *Information desk.* This is a general assistance area—the name speaks for itself. The staff at this desk will refer you to the appropriate section of the library to find particular source material or to the appropriate librarian who can answer specific questions of yours. While you are here, find out what days and hours the library is open.

- *Reference desk.* The staff at this desk are true generalists, who can answer all manner of questions or point you to sources that will help you answer them. They will probably ask you to make use of general reference works (such as *Psychological Abstracts* or *Social Sciences Citation Index*) at desks or tables within this section, because this material is usually not circulated. If your library has a computer terminal for an on-line bibliographic search, ask the reference staff for information about the use of this resource, including how much it will cost.

- *Catalog desk.* This is the heart of the library; the card catalog is usually located nearby. The staff at this desk can provide assistance on how to use the card catalog if you have any questions after reading this chapter.

The Card Catalog

The card catalog is a file of alphabetized 3 x 5-inch index cards or, in some libraries, a computerized catalog in a book or microfilm format of alphabetized listings. These catalogs tell you what is in the library and where to find it. Some libraries list periodicals (journals, magazines, newspapers) separately in a serials catalog. Suppose you wanted to check out a book by Robert Rosenthal and Lenore Jacobson titled *Pygmalion in the Classroom.* The library's books are usually entered on three types of catalog cards: author cards, title cards, and subject cards. If you looked in the card catalog under either "Rosenthal, Robert" or "Jacobson, Lenore" (author cards) or *"Pygmalion in the Classroom"* (title card), you would find a **call number** indicating where this book was located in the library's stacks (the rows of shelving throughout the library). The stacks are numbered according to general categories, and these coincide with the numbers and letters on the index card in the card catalog. The call number also appears at the bottom of the spine of the book.

With few exceptions, each item held by the library (textbooks, reference works, phonograph records, tapes, films, and so on) has a catalog card that gives a full description of the material and its call number. To find out whether your library has the work you are looking for, you need only the name of one of the authors or the title of the work. Without such information, you could also search through the appropriate subject cards until you located the work in question.

The author card for Rosenthal and Jacobson's *Pygmalion in the Classroom* is shown in Exhibit 1. It shows the name and birth year of the first author (Rosenthal, Robert, 1933–). Below this is the title of the work and its subtitle (teacher expectation and pupils' intellectual development), followed by the complete list of authors in the order in which they appear on the title page of the work. Then follows the location and name of the publisher (New York, Holt, Rinehart and Winston) and the date of copyright (1968).

In the upper-left corner of the card is the call number—a sequence of letters and numbers specified by the Library of Congress to identify this particular work. The Library of Congress classification system uses letter designations for various subjects: A for general works, B for philosophy and religion, H for social science, L for education, and so on. If your library allows students to have access to the stacks, then you would first go to the LB section and next to the more specific section in numeric (1131) and then alphanumeric order (R585) where Rosenthal and Jacobson's book was shelved.

The remainder of the catalog card contains further technical facts about this work. The information noted in the middle of the card informs us of the number of

8

```
LB        Rosenthal, Robert, 1933—
1131          Pygmalion in the classroom; teacher expectation and pupils'
R585      intellectual  development  [by]  Robert  Rosenthal  [and]  Lenore
          Jacobson.  New York, Holt, Rinehart and Winston [1968]
              xi, 240 p. illus. 23 cm
              Bibliography: p. 219–229.


              1. Prediction of scholastic success. 2. Mental tests.  I.
          Jacobson, Lenore, joint author.  II. Title.

          LB1131.R585          372.1'2'644          68–19667

          Library of Congress
```

Exhibit 1 Sample catalog card

prefatory pages in this book (xi) and the length of the book (240 p.); it also indicates that the book contains figures or other illustrations (illus.), that it stands 23 cm. high on the shelf, and that the bibliography is on pages 219 to 229. The section below that indicates the categories under which this book is cataloged ("Mental tests," for example). Next is the book's Library of Congress classification number again (LB1131.R585), the Dewey Decimal classification number of this work (372.1'2'644), the order number of this particular set of catalog cards (68–19667), and from whom they can be ordered (Library of Congress).

The Dewey Decimal classification system is an alternative to the Library of Congress classification system for cataloging material. Both proceed from general classification letters or numbers to more specific call numbers so that the material you want can be located in only one place in the stacks. The Dewey Decimal classification system uses three-digit number designations: 000 for general works, 100 for philosophy, 300 for social sciences, 500 for pure science, 900 for history and biography, and so on.

Beginning a Literature Search

Let us explore some ways you might look for literature related to your research or term paper topic. You can do a by-hand search if all you need are key studies and do not want to pay for a computer literature search, or you can order an on-line search if you want to save time or need to compile a comprehensive bibliography of relatively recent studies. Even with an on-line computer search of the literature, you will still need to manually weed out irrelevant material.

Suppose all you need are four or five key citations to provide the basis for a working hypothesis in the introductory section of a research report. A good place to look for key studies is the reference or bibliography section of a standard text, sourcebook, or annual review. Another source of references on specific topics is the *Psychological Bulletin*, a journal of literature reviews; the last issue of every volume has an index. However, do not just lift citations of articles or your instructor may wonder if you have even read the study cited.

Ask your instructor for some leads before you exhaust yourself searching aimlessly in the library for just the right reference or bibliography section. The catalog card in Exhibit 1 notes that Rosenthal and Jacobson's book contains an eleven-page bibliography—certainly a likely place to begin a search for key studies if you were writing a paper on the effects of expectations among people. With Rosenthal and Jacobson's bibliography section in hand, you might track down four or five key works by comparing bibliographies from other books with Rosenthal and Jacobson's to find out what books or journal articles were routinely cited.

Incidentally, if you happen to be looking for a reference book about reference books in your field, ask an information librarian for E. P. Sheehy's *Guide to Reference Books*. This is a comprehensive annotated listing of reference books. If you simply ask for "Sheehy's," the librarian will know what you mean and will point you to the reference section of the library (if you have not already located it). There are also many other good bibliographies (and many less a librarian's tool than Sheehy's is) to which an information librarian should be able to refer students. A librarian friend of ours reminds us to emphasize that information librarians are highly skilled in putting students on the right track to finding material for writing a paper. No matter how much paperwork the librarian has on the desk, and no matter how busy the librarian looks, students should not be intimidated. Do not be afraid to approach an information librarian for help, because that is the librarian's main purpose.

Indexes and Abstracts

Besides textbooks, sourcebooks, and annuals, other sources of key references are indexes and abstracts, such as *Social Sciences Citation Index* or *Science Citation Index* (whichever is more appropriate to your task) and *Psychological Abstracts*.

Social Sciences Citation Index (SSCI) is a continuously updated series of volumes consisting of three separate, but related, encyclopedic indexes to the behavioral science literature dating back to 1966. Suppose you found an interesting article or book published in 1968. Its reference list sends you to related publications from 1968 and earlier. To find more recent publications on the topic, the particular *SSCI* index that you would consult is the citation index. It shows, in alphabetical order by first author's last name, the year's published literature that cited the work. If you looked up Rosenthal and Jacobson's 1968 book, *Pygmalion in the Classroom*, in the 1984 *SSCI* citation index, you would find under Robert Rosenthal's name the list of citations shown in Exhibit 2. Each entry refers to a work that makes reference to this book (for example, Anderson, K. M.), the source of the work (*Elementary School Journal*), the volume number (84), then the beginning page number (315) and year of publication (1984). You can go to the periodicals section of your library and examine references such as Anderson's article to see whether they are germane to your project.

68 PYGMALION CLASSROOM

		VOL	PG	YR
ANDERSON KM	ELEM SCH J	84	315	84
BALL DW	PSYCHOL REP	54	347	84
BLANCK PD	J EDUC PSYC	76	418	84
BROPHY J	CC/SOC BEH		16	84
BUGENTAL DB	MON S RES C	49	1	84
CADMAN D	AM J PUB HE	74	1093	84
CARROLL JL	PSYCHOL SCH	21	343	84
COLVIN M	AM J SOCIOL	89	513	83
COOPER HM	ELEM SCH J	85	77	84
CORSON D	"	84	458	84
EDEN D	ACAD MGMT R	9	64	84
EHRENWAL J	J AM S PSYC	78	29	84
ERWIN PG	BR J ED PSY	54	223	84
GRIM P	NEW IDEA PS	2	35	84
HENDRICK I	J AS STUD P	18	3	83
KARPER WB	EDUC RES Q	8	40	83
LEMIRE G	CAN J CRIM	26	459	84
MARSHALL HH	REV EDUC RE	54	301	84
MARTIN DS	J REHABIL D	17	17	84
MARTINEK TJ	J SPORT PSY	6	408	84
"	RES Q EXERC	55	32	84
MCGOWAN RJ	HISPAN J B	6	205	84
MCWHIRTE JJ	PERS GUID J	62	580	84
MOULDEN M	ENVIR PL A	16	49	84
PROCTOR CP	ELEM SCH J	84	469	84
RAMPAUL WE	ALBER J EDU	30	213	84
RAUDENBU SW	J EDUC PSYC	76	85	84
RICHEY LS	J LEARN DI	16	610	83
ROSENTHA R	J CONS CLIN	52	679	84
SAFRAN SP	LEARN DISAB	7	102	84
SCHWARZW J	MEGAMOT	28	207	84
SMEAD VS	ALBER J EDU	30	145	84
STRYKER S	ADV EXP SOC	16	181	83
SWANN WB	J PERS SOC	46	1267	84
"	PSYCHOL REV	91	457	84
TSUI AS	ORGAN BEH H	34	64	84
WATSON W	SOCIAL SC M	19	629	84

Exhibit 2 Sample citations from *SSCI*

Psychological Abstracts, a periodical published by the American Psychological Association, gives synopses of thousands of works in psychology and related disciplines. Exhibit 3 reproduces four abstracts from a volume of *Psychological Abstracts* published in 1984 (volume 71): an article criticizing another article; a theoretical paper in a foreign journal; a research study on animal behavior; and a literature review. Each abstract contains information about the particular work. For instance, Baumrind's abstract begins with a *Psychological Abstracts* code number (13800), so you can easily find the abstract again by going back to this volume and looking up this number. The author's name is then listed; if there were more than four authors, the first author would be listed followed by *et al.* The first author's affiliation is given next, and then the work's title is shown, followed by the journal (or other) source where the work appeared. If the work is written in a foreign language (as in the abstract of Berndt de Souza Mello's work in Portuguese), then the original title would be followed by the translated title. A synopsis of the work follows; next are the number of references and the source of the abstract.

Psychological Abstracts covers the period from 1927 to the present. Other useful abstracts in psychology and education include *Sociological Abstracts* (1952 to present), *ERIC* (Education Resources Information Center), and the often overlooked *Social Sciences Index* (1974 to present). There are abstracts and indexes for just about every discipline and area of interest (*Biological Abstracts, Art Index, Abridged Index Medicus, Humanities Index*), and an information librarian will direct you to

13800. Baumrind, Diana. (U California, Inst of Human Development, Berkeley) **Specious causal attributions in the social sciences: The reformulated stepping-stone theory of heroin use as exemplar.** *Journal of Personality & Social Psychology,* 1983(Dec), Vol 45(6), 1289–1298.
—Examines the claims based on causal models employing either statistical or experimental controls. Such claims were found to be excessive when applied to social or behavioral science data. An exemplary case, in which strong causal claims are made on the basis of a weak version of the regularity model of cause, is critiqued. J. A. O'Donnell and R. R. Clayton (see PA, Vol 70:12937) claim that to establish that marihuana use is a cause of heroin use (their "reformulated stepping-stone" hypothesis), it is necessary and sufficient to demonstrate that marihuana use precedes heroin use and that the statistically significant association between use of the 2 drugs does not vanish when the effects of other variables deemed to be prior to both of them are removed. Here, it is argued that O'Donnell and Clayton's version of the regularity model is not sufficient to establish cause and that the planning of social interventions both presumes and requires a generative rather than a regularity causal model. Causal modeling using statistical controls is of value when it compels the investigator to make explicit and to justify a causal explanation but not when it is offered as a substitute for a generative analysis of causal connection. (41 ref) —*Journal abstract.*

14246. Searcy, William A. (U Pittsburgh) **Response to multiple song types in male song sparrows and field sparrows.** *Animal Behaviour,* 1983(Aug), Vol 31(3), 948–949.
—Examined whether J. R. Kreb's (1977) hypothesis, which proposes that song repertoires in birds function in territorial defense, can explain interspecific differences in repertoire size. 30 male field sparrows (*Spizella pursilla*) and 30 male song sparrows (*Melospiza melodia*) were tested. Contrary to predictions, male field sparrows, which lack repertoires, showed a preferential response to multiple song types, while male song sparrows, which possess repertoires, did not. It is concluded that Kreb's hypothesis does not explain the interspecific difference in repertoire size in these sparrows. (7 ref)

15519. Berndt de Souza Mello, Jansy. Dois triângulos. [Two triangles.] (Port) *Alter-Jornal de Estudos Psicodinâmicos,* 1980(Jan–Dec), Vol 10(1–3), 77–82.
—Relationships in the Oedipus myth can be seen as a triangle of father, mother, and child, one member being excluded from the opposite pair. The present author contends that the psycholanalyst–patient relationship can be thought of as a triangle formed by the patient, the patient's memories and emotions, and the analyst with his/her outside perspective. In the transference relationship the analyst may be included in the patient's memories. An analyst, excluding him/herself may interrupt the patient to aid progress to a more human and realistic relationship. In a clinical example, a patient simultaneously addresses an analyst both as a real person and, in the transference relationship, as a loved one. (English abstract) (4 ref) —*G. L. Chesnut.*

14747. Epstein, Joyce L. (Johns Hopkins U, Ctr for Social Organization of Schools) **Choice of friends over the life span: Developmental and environmental influences.** *Center for Social Organization of Schools Report, Johns Hopkins U.,* 1983(Jul), Rpt No 345, 96 p.
—Presents a life-course perspective on the selection of friends. Research results on 3 aspects of the selection process are discussed: (1) facts of selection—the number of friends and their proximity; (2) the surface of selection—the visible features of friends such as their sex, race, and age; and (3) the depth of selection—characteristics of friendships and similarity of friends. Over 250 references are reviewed to learn how patterns of selection change with age and under different environmental conditions from preschool to postsecondary school settings. The research reveals important developmental patterns in the selection of friends. With age and with the development of cognitive skills and experiences, older students tend to choose fewer best friends, make choices from wider boundaries, increase cross-sex choices, decrease cross-race choices, move toward mixed-age choices, reciprocate and stabilize friendships, and choose more similar friends. There are also important environmental effects on choice of friends. For example, elementary, junior high, and high schools may be organized to encourage wide or narrow contacts; to reward, ignore, or punish cross-sex, cross-race, or mixed-age choices of friends; or to emphasize differences or similarities among students. These and other environmental conditions affect selection in ways that revise expected patterns of choosing friends. Ideas for new research are presented that stress the importance of developmental and environmental factors in studies of friendship selection and influence. (15 ref) —*Journal abstract.*

Exhibit 3 Sample abstracts from *Psychological Abstracts.* These abstracts are reprinted with the permission (fee paid) of the American Psychological Association, publisher of *Psychological Abstracts* and the *PsycINFO Database* (Copyright © 1967–1984 by the American Psychological Association) and may not be reproduced without its prior written permission.

the relevant indexes and abstracts. If you would like a list of everything that is available in the way of data bases and printed abstracts and indexes in your field, see M.L.C. Rosenthal's "Bibliographic Retrieval for the Social and Behavioral Sciences" (*Research in Higher Education*, 1985, vol. 22, pp. 315–333).

Psychological Abstracts (and most other indexes) include an author index and a subject index. The author index can be useful for finding up-to-date publications by a researcher you have already identified as a leader in the area. The subject index can be valuable if used with care. Avoid looking up a broad topic that will have pages of listings. For example, to find material on learning abilities of insects, check *insects*, not *learning*.

Machine-Readable Data Bases

Unless you are writing a senior thesis and need to do an exhaustive search on a narrow topic, a literature search by hand will be adequate. However, if you need to prepare a comprehensive bibliography of relatively recent citations on a topic, then the most efficient way to approach your task is to draw on a **machine-readable data base**—computer jargon that means the file of information sought is accessible by means of a video screen or a computer printout. For this search, talk with a librarian, who will help you choose correct keywords and descriptors to facilitate retrieval of the desired literature and to exclude scores of irrelevant citations. You will be asked to pare down your topic as precisely as you can and to avoid undertaking a complete search on a broad topic. For example, if you ask for material on "social behavior in children," you may get an unmanageable printout and a big bill. Like painting a room or blacktopping a driveway, the more effort spent in conscientious preparation for the task, the better the final outcome.

Be prepared to consider the following points when you approach the librarian for assistance:

- What is the particular topic to be searched? In answering this question, use special terms as well as common words, including synonyms and alternate spellings. Answer the question as fully as possible, and define any words or phrases you use that may have special meaning within your field.
- Describe any related terms or applications in which you are *not* interested, so the computer can be instructed to discard seemingly relevant, but inappropriate, references. Your answer to this question will help reduce the cost of your computer search.
- List two or three of the most important authors on your topic. This, plus the following three points, will help the computer to zero in on your topic.
- List two or three of the most important journals in your subject.
- List two or three of the most significant articles on your topic. If you do not know enough about your subject to do this, ask your instructor for suggestions or check some recent sourcebooks or standard textbooks for clues.

- Give the time span that you would like the computer search to cover. The time span of indexes and abstracts varies widely; the librarian will tell you the years covered by the data bases to which your library subscribes.

Some Further Guidelines

Suppose you found a word or phrase that you did not understand and could not find in your desk dictionary or in the library's unabridged dictionaries. If it were a psychological term, you could look it up in any of a number of standard reference works, such as B. B. Wolman's *Dictionary of Behavioral Science*, Wolman's multivolume *International Encyclopedia of Psychiatry, Psychology, Psychoanalysis, and Neurology*, or R. J. Corsini's *Encyclopedia of Psychology*. Other useful encyclopedic works are the *International Encyclopedia of the Social Sciences* and *The Encyclopedia of Education*. The best unabridged dictionary of the English language is the multivolume *Oxford English Dictionary*, which you will find fascinating if you are interested in word origins.

Here are some other tips as you begin your literature search:

- Try to be realistic in your assessment of your literature needs. Too little work will result in a weak foundation for your project, but too much material and intemperate expectations will overwhelm you and your subject.
- How can you find out what is a happy medium between too little and too much? Talk with your instructor before you start an intensive literature search. Ask whether your plan seems realistic.
- Before you begin your literature search, ask the instructor to recommend any key works that you should read or consult. Even if you feel confident in your subject already, asking the instructor for specific leads could prevent you from going off on a tangent.
- Do not expect to finish your literature search in one sitting. If you do, you run the risk of making yourself anxious and rushing a task that should be done patiently and methodically.
- In planning your schedule, give yourself ample time to do a thorough job. Patience will pay off in making you feel more confident that you understand your topic well.
- It is not always easy to discard a study that you have made an effort to track down, but quantity should not replace quality in the studies you finally use in your research report or term paper. Your instructor wll be more impressed with a tightly reasoned paper than with one overflowing with superfluous background material.
- Suppose you cannot locate the material you are looking for in the stacks. Some students will repeatedly return to the library for days seeking a book or journal article before discovering that what they are looking for has been lost or stolen or is being rebound. Ask an information librarian to find the elusive material. If the work you need is unavailable, you might try

consulting another college library; sometimes your own college library will do this for you.

- If you are looking for a specialized work, you probably will not find it in a small public library, so do not waste your time. When students spend a lot of time off campus in public libraries and bookstores looking for source material, they usually come back with references from general texts and current mass-market periodicals.

Taking Background Notes

You need to take precise, carefully documented background notes. Having detailed notes will pay off not only as you start pulling facts and ideas together into precise sentences and paragraphs but it will also help to avoid committing **plagiarism** accidentally. Plagiarism refers to taking someone's ideas or words and representing them as your own. You plagiarize intentionally when you knowingly copy or summarize someone's work without acknowledging that source, and you plagiarize accidentally when you copy someone's work but forget to credit it or put it in quotes. Plagiarism is illegal, and you can guard against it when taking notes.

A good procedure is to use a separate index card for each quotable idea that you find as you uncover relevant material in your literature search. Many writers prefer making notes on five-by-eight-inch rather than three-by-five-inch index cards, since they can usually get all the information they want on the front of a larger card, making it easier to find what they want when they later sort through their cards. Shown in Exhibit 4 are two examples of notes taken for a term paper, where the student has found two sections in the same source for the paper.

Note that the cards are numbered in the upper right "1 of 2" and "2 of 2" and the book's call number is included in the lower left. Once you have an outline, you can also code each card (in the lower right) with the particular section of the outline that the material on the card will illustrate. In this way you can maintain a general order in your notes, so you will avoid the task of facing a huge stack of miscellaneous bits and pieces of information that will loom large as you try to sort and integrate the information into a useful form. Be consistent with all the reference numbers you decide to use on your note cards; a haphazard arrangement will only slow you down when it is time to begin writing the first draft.

These two cards contain a wealth of material. At the top of both cards is a complete citation. It will be required in your bibliography, where you list all the sources you used, and will be condensed in citations in the body of your paper. The top card summarizes in the notetaker's *own words* the major details of the study reported by Rosenthal and Jacobson. This synopsis ends with a quotation chosen to illustrate the authors' conclusions. Note that the page number of the quote is included because if the student decides to use this quote, the page number must be cited. On the bottom card, the student has focused the material taken from this book by asking a particular question. The lengthy quotation copied from the book specifically addresses the question. Note that four dots (an ellipsis plus a period) interrupt the text halfway through the quote; they indicate that a portion of the quote has been purposely omitted.

Rosenthal, Robert, and Jacobson, Lenore (1968). *Pygmalion in the classroom: Teacher expectation and pupils' intellectual development.* New York: Holt, Rinehart and Winston

Teachers at "Oak School" (an elementary school in California) were led to believe that about 20% of students were potential "bloomers" based on their performance on a test to pick out intellectual bloomers (or spurters). Actually, the names of the 20% had been chosen at random and the test was a nonverbal IQ test (TOGA). All students were retested with TOGA after one semester, after a full academic year, and after two academic years. The IQ gains of the 20% (the experimental group) consistently surpassed the IQ gains of the remaining (control group) students. This result is consistent with Rosenthal's self-fulfilling prophecy hypothesis (see also Merton, R.). The authors conclude that "... one person's expectation for another person's behavior can quite unwittingly become a more accurate prediction simply for its having been made." (page vii)
LB1131.R585

Rosenthal, Robert, and Jacobson, Lenore (1968). *Pygmalion in the classroom: Teacher expectation and pupils' intellectual development.* New York: Holt, Rinehart and Winston.

What practical implications do these authors draw from their research findings? "As teacher-training institutions begin to teach the possibility that teachers' expectations of their pupils' performance may serve as self-fulfilling prophecies, there may be a new expectancy created. The new expectancy may be that children can learn more than had been believed possible, an expectation held by many educational theorists, though for quite different reasons.... The new expectancy, at the very least, will make it more difficult when they encounter the educationally disadvantaged for teachers to think, 'Well, after all, what can you expect?' The man on the street may be permitted his opinions and prophecies of the unkempt children loitering in a dreary schoolyard. The teacher in the schoolroom may need to learn that those same prophecies within her may be fulfilled; she is no casual passer-by. Perhaps Pygmalion in the classroom is more her role." (pp. 181-182)
LB1131.R585

Exhibit 4 Sample note cards

Library Etiquette

Before we turn to the basics of outlining the term paper (Chapter 3) or structuring the research report (Chapter 4), there is one final thing to keep in mind when using the library. The golden rule of library etiquette is to treat others as you would also have them treat you. In short, be quiet, never tear out pages, do not monopolize material, and return books and periodicals as soon as you have finished with them.

3

Outlining the Term Paper

Once you have chosen your topic and begun library work and note taking, the next step in developing the term paper will be to make an outline. The imposition of form will help you collect and refine your thoughts as you construct the paper. If you are writing a research report, you can skip this chapter and go on to Chapter 4.

Where to Start

Think of the outline as a road map to the ideas and notes you are assembling to present in your term paper. If done correctly, the outline will show a logical progression of the points of interest that the paper will cover. Initially, a tentative and general outline might be generated as you use the library's resources—a kind of shopping list for quotes and reference material that will serve to flesh out the paper when the time comes to sit down and write.

If you find it difficult to begin writing, a good quotation can sometimes launch the discussion that your term paper will have as its core. Ask yourself the reporter's questions: who, what, where, when, and why? Use comparison and contrast as a way of structuring the outline in your mind, or if you have a thesis, begin by outlining it and then use specific facts and studies as subtopics to document it in this preliminary outline. Before you begin writing, however, you will want to revise the tentative working outline so that it reflects the organizational structure you will use to shape the term paper.

Making Ideas Parallel

Outline items can be set down in three different forms, using either topics, sentences, or paragraphs. The specific form chosen should be the only one used in the outline, so that all the ideas are parallel. In the following outline fragment (which uses the term paper in Appendix A for background information), the ideas clearly are not parallel:

I. Definition
   A. Adolescent females as victims of disorder
   B. Symptoms
      1. weight loss
      2. patient has a distorted body image
      3. amenorrhea
   C. Psychological aspects of the disorder include:
      1. perfectionist's disease
      2. high achievers

The problem with the preceding outline is that it is a hodgepodge of topics and sentences. Working with this jumble is like swimming upstream. Such an outline will only sabotage your efforts to put thoughts and notes into a logical sequence. Contrast this inconsistent structure with the parallel structure of the following format, which is based on the same background information in Maria's paper:

I. Define anorexia nervosa
   A. Disorder that occurs mainly in adolescent females
   B. Physical symptoms include:
      1. loss of at least 25 percent of body weight
      2. distorted body image
      3. possible presence of amenorrhea
   C. Psychological symptoms include:
      1. anorectics desire perfection
      2. anorectics tend to be high achievers

Putting Ideas in Order

Whether you use topics, sentences, or paragraphs for your outline, group your information from the most general facts or ideas in descending order to the most specific details and examples. We see this clearly in the parallel format of the outline shown immediately above. As the following example illustrates, the same rule applies whether we are outlining definitions and symptoms or the nature of a specific therapeutic approach in a clinical investigation that we plan to elaborate in our first draft:

III. Therapeutic approaches to anorexia nervosa
   A. Lucas, Duncan, & Piens (1976)
      1. separate anorectic from family
      2. institute weight gain program
      3. use psychotherapy for patient
      4. use family therapy for patient's family
   B. Andersen (personal communication)
      1. begin nutritional restitution
      2. administer individual therapy
      3. give patient increased responsibilities
      4. use follow-ups to guard against relapse

Another rule to keep in mind is that there should be two or more subtopics under any topic. That is, if you list I, you should list II; if A, then B; if 1, then 2, and so on. To clarify division of the material and the order of the ideas in the outline, its parts are systematically labeled and indented as follows:

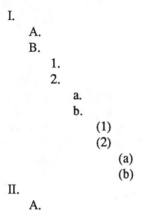

I.
  A.
  B.
    1.
    2.
      a.
      b.
        (1)
        (2)
          (a)
          (b)
II.
  A.

The roman numerals indicate the outline's main ideas. Indented capital letters provide main divisions within the groups of main ideas. The letters and numbers that follow list the supporting details and examples. Note the indentation of each subtopic. Note also that there are at least two items under all headings; any of these categories can be expanded to fit the number of supporting details or examples that you wish to cover in the term paper. The use of roman numerals I, II, III, capitals A, B, C, arabic numerals 1, 2, 3, small letters a, b, c, and finally numbers and letters in parentheses serves as a means of classifying facts, ideas, and concepts. Lapses of logic, if there are any, are bound to surface if this system of organization is used, so you can easily catch and correct them before proceeding.

For example, look at the following abbreviated outline; the entry labeled "C" is a conspicuous lapse in logic:

I. Symptoms
    A. weight loss
    B. amenorrhea
    C. use psychotherapy for patient
    D. distorted body image

Item C should be moved from this section of the outline to the section pertaining to therapeutic approaches to anorexia nervosa. Another instance might require a return to the library to clarify a point or to fill in with the appropriate reference material. If you carefully work out and revise your outline, actual writing becomes simply the fleshing out of the basic structure.

Further Helpful Hints

If you find it difficult to start writing, then making a sentence outline first may be the perfect way to begin. With the sentence outline format, the paper will almost write itself.

3 / Outlining the Term Paper

Here is a fragment of a sentence outline; as you can see, all that is needed are some transitions and polishing:

I. Anorexia nervosa is the technical term for a psychological disorder characterized by lack of appetite and inability to eat.
  A. There are a number of recognizable physical and psychological symptoms, which include
    1. the loss of at least 25 percent of original weight;
    2. cessation or delay of the menstrual period (amenorrhea) in women;
    3. the self-perception of being layered in fat, in spite of the victim's emaciated appearance.

There is one other helpful hint about using an outline that we alluded to in Chapter 2. The outline's coding system makes it convenient to code the notes you took during your literature search. If the notes on an index card pertain to section "II.B.1." of your outline, then you would code this information on the card. In this way, order is brought to the stack of index cards that you have accumulated. If you spread them out on the floor and sort and code them according to the section of the outline they pertain to, the paper will take shape from notes and the outline, each component enhancing the other. Keep in mind that the outline is only a guide, and its form will probably change as the process of integrating notes and outline proceeds.

Outlining After the Fact

Some people find the process of making an outline too exacting, preferring instead to sit at the typewriter or word processor, or with pencil in hand, so that the ideas can flow naturally. An experienced writer working with a particular subject can sometimes achieve success with this unstructured approach, but for others the results can create havoc and frustration.

However, if you feel that you do not have the self-discipline to make an outline at the outset, at least make one later. To assure yourself that your work has a coherent form—what psychologists call a "good gestalt"—see if you can outline your first draft after the fact if you did not make an outline beforehand. Ask yourself:

- Is the discussion focused, and do the ideas flow from or build on one another?
- Is there ample development of each idea?
- Are there supporting details for each main idea discussed?
- Are the ideas balanced?
- Is the writing to the point, or has it gone off on a tangent?

If you would like to practice on someone else's work, try making an outline of Maria's term paper. Ask yourself how well her paper satisfies the various criteria addressed in the five preceding questions. If you discover problems with the structure of this term paper, try to think of ways that she could have avoided them or corrected them after the first draft.

4

Planning the Research Report

As noted in Chapter 1, the research report has a structure in which data form the core of the report and your literature review usually involves only a few key studies that give a basis to your working hypothesis. This chapter deals with the structure and form of research reports. If you are writing a term paper, you can go on to Chapter 5.

The Basic Structure

By now, course work and your instructor's recommendations should have led you through the process of narrowing your area of interest so that your study is feasible and your methods and procedures are appropriate to your study. Many texts cover data collection and data analysis. We will assume that you have mastered the relevant techniques they describe, so that the remaining task is to plan a clear, concise report.

Reexamine John's research report in Appendix B and you will see that it has eight parts:

- Title page
- Abstract
- Introduction
- Method
- Results
- Discussion
- References
- Appendix

Except for the layout of the title page and the addition of the appendix in this report, the structure corresponds generally to the standardized format recommended by the *Publication Manual of the American Psychological Association* (third edition). The title page is straightforward, so we will focus on the remaining seven parts of the research report.

Abstract

Although the abstract comes at the beginning of your report, it is actually written after you complete the rest of your paper. The abstract provides a concise summary of your report. Think of it as a distillation of the important points covered in the body of the report. Thus in the sample research report, John gives a synopsis of his hypothesis, the methodology of the investigation, and the results in one succinct paragraph.

When planning your abstract, here are some questions for you to answer as concisely as possible:

- What was the objective or purpose of the research study?
- What principal method was used?
- Who were the research participants?
- What were the major results?
- What was the central conclusion?

More detailed and more specific statements about methods, results, and conclusions are treated in the body of your report. The brief summary of the abstract tells the instructor what your report is about.

Introduction

The introduction to your research report should give a concise history and background of your topic. In the sample report, John has chosen to introduce his project by defining the term that forms the basis of his study. In this way, the reader is given a general fact needed to appreciate and assess John's work. He then cites specific studies to provide the reader with additional background on the topic and then concludes his introduction with a statement of his hypothesis, thereby leading us easily into the next section of the report.

Generally speaking, the introduction provides the rationale for your study and prepares the reader for the methods that you chose to accomplish the research. The literature review shows the development of your hypothesis and the reason you believe the research question to be important. The strongest introductions are those that describe the research question or hypothesis posed in such a way that the methods section appears to be a natural consequence of that question or hypothesis. If you can get readers to think when they later read your methods section, "Yes, of course, that's what this researcher had to do to answer the question," you will have written a strong introduction.

Here are some questions to ask yourself as you plan this section:

- What was the purpose of your study?
- What terms need to be defined?
- How does the study build on, or derive from, other studies?
- What was the hypothesis or expectation?

Method

The next step is to detail exactly the methods and procedures used. Care should be taken to describe fully the subject pool: age, sex, and numbers, as well as the way in which they were selected and any other details that would help to specify them. If you recruited participants from an available subject pool, tell how many of the potential subjects actually volunteered. If you happen to know something about the demographics of the subjects who did not volunteer (the nonrespondents), plan to report this information as well, perhaps in a table that compares the characteristics of the respondents and nonrespondents.

Also included in this section should be a description of the tests and measurements that you chose to use and the context in which they were presented. John Yost's report describes the questionnaire that he used and the instructions given to the participants; additionally, he notes that the subject pool was assured that their responses would remain anonymous. If you used well-known, standardized tests (TAT or MMPI, for example), it is a good idea to describe them in two or three sentences (even though in articles in professional journals naming them is usually adequate). By describing them, you communicate to your instructor that you truly understand the nature and purpose of the test you chose.

Results

In the next major section, describe your findings. You might plan to show the results in a table or figure, as in the sample report in Appendix B. Do not make your instructor guess what you are doing; label your table or figure fully and discuss the data in the prose of this section so that it is clear what the numbers represent.

The results section should consist of a careful, detailed analysis that strikes a balance between being discursive and being falsely or needlessly precise. You are guilty of **false precision** when something inherently vague is presented in overly precise terms. Suppose you asked research participants to state their opinions on a number of controversial topics using a five-point scale of "strongly agree" to "strongly disagree." It would be falsely precise to report the results to a high number of decimal places, because your measuring instrument is relatively insensitive to slight variations in opinions. You are guilty of **needless precision** when (almost without thinking about it) you report something much more exactly than the circumstances require. For example, reporting the weight of mouse subjects to six decimal places might be within the bounds of your measuring instrument, but the situation does not call for such exactitude.

Ask yourself the following questions as you structure this section:

- What did I find?
- How can I say what I found in a careful, detailed way?
- Is what I am planning to say precise and to the point?
- Am I being overly or misleadingly exact?
- Will what I have said be clear to the reader?
- Have I left anything of importance out?

Discussion

The discussion section is where you will pull together the various sections of the report to form a cohesive unit from the facts that you have gathered. A review of the introductory section is often helpful. Think about how you will discuss your research findings in light of your original hypothesis. Did serendipity (felicitous or accidental findings) play a role in the study? If so, detail the unexpected by-products and ideas they generated.

Try to write defensively, that is, to be your own devil's advocate. In other words, you should look for shortcomings or critical inconsistencies and anticipate the reader's reaction to them. Here are some further questions to consider as you begin to structure this section:

- What was the purpose of this study?
- How do my results relate to that purpose?
- Did I make any serendipitous findings of interest?
- How valid and generalizable are my findings?
- Are there larger implications in these findings?

You might wish to plan a separate conclusions section if you feel more comfortable with that format or have a lot to cover that you would like to separate from the main body of your discussion. However, it is quite proper to treat the final paragraph or two of your discussion section as the conclusion. In either case, your conclusions should be stated as clearly and concisely as possible. If there are larger implications, spell them out. Are there implications for further research? If so, suggest them here. In the discussion section of the sample report, John Yost generalizes from the specific results that his study has yielded. He has structured his report to combine the discussion and conclusion and has included a closing paragraph on the implications for future research.

References

Once you have made plans for writing the body of the report, give some thought to your reference material again. You will need to include an alphabetized listing of all the sources of information on which you drew. To avoid having to retrace your steps, keep a running list of the material that will appear in this section as you progress through the early preparation of the report. If you make a separate index card for each reference that you actually use in your report, it will be a simple matter later to alphabetize the cards and make sure that none have been omitted.

Appendix

The purpose of this final section is to display the raw materials and computations of your investigation, for example, any questionnaires or tests that you constructed but did not fully document in the main body of your report. In the sample report, John includes his statistical calculations. Your instructor may wish to waive the requirement of an appendix, or may stipulate a different list of items to be included. In case your instructor has questions about your findings, be sure to keep all of your notes and data until the instructor returns your report.

Getting Going

Before we conclude this discussion about planning the basic elements of your report, we want to add a word about how to get going. In the preceding chapter, we discussed how to go about making an outline for the term paper; the research report does not require an outline because its formal structure already provides a skeleton waiting to be fleshed out. Nevertheless, most researchers find it helpful to organize their thoughts about each section before writing the first draft.

There are several alternative ways to begin. If you like to work with a detailed sentence outline, then read Chapter 3 for guidelines. Another possibility is to make notes on separate index cards for each major point—rationale of the study, derivation of each hypothesis, and each background study, for example—and draw on these notes to write your first draft. Some researchers find it helpful to take notes on yellow pads and then catalog their pages in separate file folders corresponding to each major section of their report. No matter what approach you favor, make sure that your notes are accurate and complete. If you are summarizing someone else's study, you must note the full citation. If you are quoting someone, include the statement in quotes and make sure that you have copied it exactly. The process of taking notes and ordering them will help you to reorganize the sections of your report into a cohesive unit directing the flow of your writing.

5

Writing and Revising

Writing a first draft is a little like taking the first dip into chilly ocean waters on a hot day. It may be uncomfortable at the outset, but feels better once you get used to it. In this chapter we provide some general pointers to buoy you up as you begin.

Focusing on the Objective

At this stage of your work, you should have an ordered set of notes and either an outline, in the case of a term paper, or a given structure if your project is a research report. The material you have assembled can be thought of as the bare bones of the paper. Sentences and paragraphs will now be combined to fill out the skeleton.

To begin writing the first draft, write down somewhere the purpose or goal you have in mind. Make this self-motivator statement succinct so you have a focus for your thoughts as you begin to set them down on paper.

If we refer to the two sample papers, we can imagine the following self-motivators:

From Maria

I'm planning a paper that will discuss the difference between two modes of treatment for anorexia nervosa.

From John

My research report will answer the question: Are people more likely to transmit rumors that they believe to be true or rumors they don't believe to be true?

This trick can help to keep your mind focused so that writing the paper does not seem like such a formidable task. You will be less apt to wander off on a tangent.

Settling Down to Write

Should you find yourself having trouble starting, try the trick of not beginning at the opening of your paper. Start writing whatever section you feel will be easiest, and then tackle the rest as your ideas begin to flow. When faced with the blank page, some students escape by taking a nap or watching television. Recognize these counterproductive moves for what they are and avoid them.

The following pointers are general hints to ensure that your writing will go as smoothly as possible:

- While writing, try to work in a quiet, well-lighted place in two-hour stretches.
- If you are typing your first draft, double- or triple-space it so you will have room for legible revisions. If you are writing on a note pad, skip a line for each line you write down.
- Be sure to number the pages as you write, to maintain order and keep track of your efforts.
- When you take a break, try to stop at a point that is halfway through an idea or a paragraph. In this way you can resume work where you left off and avoid feeling stuck or having to start cold.
- Try to pace your work so that you can complete the first draft and let it rest for twenty-four hours. When you return to the completed first draft after a break, your own critical powers will be enhanced and you will have a fresh approach to the shaping of the final draft.

Before you start writing, let's return to the subject of plagiarism mentioned briefly in Chapter 2.

Plagiarism and Lazy Writing

It is crucial that students understand what constitutes plagiarism and what consequences result for those who fall into it. As any member of a college faculty will tell you, plagiarism is the unacknowledged use of the ideas or words of another. Failure to cite borrowed ideas is plagiarism. This does not mean, however, that you cannot ask an interested friend or parent to read and comment on the rough draft of your paper. If you do, mention that person's help in a preface to the paper or in a footnote acknowledgment. (But use footnotes sparingly; numerous footnotes suggest that you do not understand how to reference.)

Lazy students, upon hearing that quotations and citations are not construed by definition as plagiarism, sometimes submit papers consisting almost entirely of quoted material. Unless you feel that it is absolutely essential, avoid quoting long passages throughout a paper. It will be necessary to quote or paraphrase some material (with a citation, of course), but your written work is expected to be the result of your own individual effort. The penalty for plagiarism is usually a failing grade in the course and a written report on the incident to the dean. The penalty for lazy writing is usually a reduced grade. Avoid both. It is a good idea to keep your note cards, outlines, and rough drafts, since some instructors will ask students for such material if a question arises about the originality of the work.

Especially when dealing with technical material, many students use terms that they do not understand—anatomical terms, for example. Although this is not considered plagiarism, it constitutes lazy writing. Always make your point in your own words. If you cannot say it in your own words, then you do not understand it well enough to write about it.

Tone

As you write, there are style points to be kept in mind. A classic reference source that you may find useful is W. Strunk, Jr., and E. B. White's *The Elements of Style* (Macmillan). Here we will survey some basic style issues. The way in which your paper approaches its audience is its tone. Your writing should not be dull; presumably you are writing on a topic that you find fascinating, since you chose it. Strive for an explicit, straightforward, interesting but not emotional way of expressing your thoughts, findings, and conclusions. Avoid having your term paper or research report read like a letter to a favorite aunt ("Here's what Jones and Smith say. . . ." or "So I told the research participants. . . ."). Do not try to duplicate a journalist's slick "newspeak" style, familiar in *Time* magazine or the glib spoken reports that network TV sometimes espouses. There is nothing wrong with using the first person ("I shall discuss. . . ." or "My conclusion is that. . . ."), but unless you have a split personality and both of you collaborate on the paper, do not refer to yourself as *we* ("We observed that. . . ." or "In this paper we will explore. . . .").

Strive for an objective, direct tone that keeps your reader subordinate to the material you are presenting. Do not write: "The reader will note that the results were. . . ." Instead, write: "The results were. . . ."

Study the following sentences lifted from our sample papers to see how the tone the author uses can color the impact of the paper. John states his hypothesis in response to a question he poses that piques our interest. He uses the impersonal pronoun *one* to make a general statement, and he avoids the awkward *he/she* or *s/he* contraction that inexperienced writers often use. Maria, on the other hand, uses the first person *I* to draw the reader into her paper. She then describes the problem in a tone that is compelling but not melodramatic or slick:

From John's research report

> "Why is it that some rumors are transmitted with greater alacrity than others during stressful situations? In this study it was hypothesized that the more confidence one has in the truth of a rumor, the more likely one is to transmit the rumor."

From Maria's term paper

> "In this paper I shall concentrate on the treatment of anorexia nervosa. The victims of this illness literally starve themselves. This results in dramatic weight losses and can even lead to death. However, in spite of their

emaciated appearance, they perceive themselves as layered in fat, a condition that they abhor and try desperately to change."

Gender

In the 1980s, the question of word gender has become a matter of some sensitivity among writers, especially those working in psychology and education. In the interests of equality of the sexes, as well as precision in writing, it is well for the student writer to avoid the archaic use of the masculine gender in nouns and pronouns when referring to both men and women—for example, "man and his world" when you mean "people and their world."

Beware of masculine nouns and pronouns that can give a sex bias to your writing that you do not intend. A way to avoid this problem is to resort to plural pronouns when possible, for example, "They did. . . ." instead of "He did. . . ." or ". . . to them" instead of ". . . to him." Use masculine and feminine pronouns when the situation calls for them. If the study you are discussing used only male research participants, then the masculine pronoun *he* is more precise than *he/she* or *s/he*, or the plural *they* that misleads the reader into thinking that the research participants were of both sexes.

Voice

The verb forms you choose to use in your writing can speak with one of two voices—active or passive. You write in the **active voice** when you represent the subject of your sentence as performing the action expressed by your verb ("The research participants responded by. . . ."). You write in the **passive voice** when the subject of your sentence undergoes the action expressed by your verb ("The response made by the research participants was. . . ."). If you rely mainly on the active voice, you will have a more vital, readable style:

Active voice

Dollard and Miller theorize that frustration leads to aggression.

Passive voice

It is theorized by Dollard and Miller that frustration leads to aggression.

However, the passive voice is often useful to avoid the gender traps of singular masculine pronouns when you actually mean to refer to both sexes. For example:

Active (gender trap)

If the subject reacted in this way, it was taken to be a clear indication of *his* provivisectionist attitude.

Passive (no gender trap)

A provivisectionist attitude was clearly indicated by the subject's reaction.

Tense

The verb tenses you use in your paper can get into a tangle unless you observe a few basic rules:

- Use the past tense to report studies that have been done in the past ("Jones and Smith found. . . ."). If you are writing a research report, your method section and results section both call for the past tense because the study has already been completed ("Rumors *were collected.* . . .").

- Use the present tense to define terms ("Rumor *is* defined as. . . ."). The present tense is also often used to state a general hypothesis ("The amount of rumor in circulation *is* equal to. . . .").

- The future tense can be saved for the section of your paper in which you discuss implications for further investigation ("Future research *will be* necessary. . . ."), though you can also discuss future implications in the present tense ("More longitudinal studies *are* needed. . . .").

Agreement of Subject and Verb

As you write, make sure each sentence expresses a complete thought. That is, it should have a subject (in general terms, something that performs the action) and a verb (an action to perform or a state of being):

Subject and verb agree

    Participants [*subject*] were [*verb*] faculty members.

Because the subject was plural (*participants*), the verb form used (*were*) was also plural. That means the verb and subject agree, a basic rule of grammar. In some sentence forms, achieving this agreement is a simple matter. However, trouble can arise in several instances:

- When you use collective nouns (those that name a group), they can be either singular or plural—for example, committee, team, faculty. When you think of the group as a single unit, use a singular verb ("The administration *is* ready to settle. . . ."). Plurals are called for when you want to refer to the components of a group ("The faculty *were* divided on the strike issue. . . .").

- Trouble can ensue when words come between subject and verb: "Therapy [*singular subject*], in combination with behavioral organic methods of weight gain, exemplifies [*singular verb form*] this approach." It would be incorrect, however, to write: "Therapy, in combination with behavioral organic methods of weight gain, *exemplify* this approach."

- Another source of problems can be the correct use of the singular and plural of some familiar terms; for example:

Singular	*Plural*
analysis	analyses
anomaly	anomalies

Singular	Plural
appendix	appendixes or appendices
criterion	criteria
datum	data
hypothesis	hypotheses
phenomenon	phenomena
stimulus	stimuli

Common Usage Errors

Instructors frequently see a number of usage errors in student research reports and term papers. Listed on the inside front cover of this manual are several pairs of words that are pronounced the same (homonyms) and are often confused with one another, such as *accept* (to receive) and *except* (other than). Another pair of confusing homonyms is *affect* and *effect*. Affect, a verb, means to influence ("frustration can affect how a person behaves"); effect, a noun, means the result of something ("aggression is often an effect of frustration"). *Affect* has a special meaning when used as a noun in psychology; it is a synonym for emotion.

Perhaps the two most common usage errors, however, are the confusion of *phenomena* [*plural*] with *phenomenon* [*singular*] and the confusion of *data* [*plural*] with *datum* [*singular*]. For example, it would be incorrect to write "This [*singular pronoun*] phenomena [*plural subject*] was [*singular verb*] of interest...." or "The data [*plural subject*] indicates [*singular verb*] that...." The correct form would be: "These phenomena were...." or "This phenomenon was...." and "The data indicate...." or "The datum indicates...."

Another common usage error occurs with the words *between* and *among*. Use *between* when you are referring to two items only; use *among* when there are more than two items. It would be incorrect to write "Between the three of them...." However, it would be correct to say "The differences *between* the experimental and control conditions were significant at...." or "Age and educational level *among* the four groups of respondents indicate...." (There is, however, one anachronism that you cannot do anything about. In the analysis of variance, conventional usage is to speak of the "between sum of squares" and "between mean square" even when the number of conditions being compared is more than two.)

Another problem concerns the confusion of the prefixes *inter-* and *intra-*. *Inter-* means between (interpersonal, or between persons); *intra-* means within (intrapersonal, or within the person). Other often troublesome prefixes are the following:

- The prefix *intro-* means inward or within, and the prefix *extra-* means outside or beyond. The psychological term *introverted* thus denotes an inner-directed personality, and *extraverted* indicates an outer-directed personality.

- The prefix *hyper-* means too much, whereas the prefix *hypo-* means too little. Hence, the term *hypothyroidism* refers to a deficiency of thyroid hormone.

Punctuation

Correct use of the various punctuation marks will ensure that your writing is clear. A period ends a declarative sentence and follows an abbreviation, as in the following common abbreviations of Latin words:

cf.	from *confer* ("compare")
e.g.	from *exempli gratia* ("for example")
et al.	from *et alia* ("and others")
ibid.	from *ibidem* ("in the same place")
i.e.	from *id est* ("that is")
op. cit.	from *opere citato* ("in the work cited")

If you continually wrote *eg.* or *et. al.* in your paper, this would be a sure sign to your instructor that you do not know the full meaning of these terms, since *e.g.* is the abbreviation for two words (not one) and *et* is not an abbreviation at all.

The several different uses of the comma include the following:

- Use commas to separate items in a series ("Smith, Jones, and Brown" or "high, medium, and low scorers").

- Set off introductory phrases in a sentence with a comma ("In a follow-up experiment performed ten years later, the same researchers did. . . .").

- Use commas to set off thoughts or phrases that are not essential to qualify the meaning of the sentence ("This variable, which was also studied by Kimmel (1982), was hypothesized to be linearly related to. . . .").

- Put a comma before connecting words (*and, but, or, nor, yet*) when they join independent clauses ("The subject lost weight, yet he was still able to. . . .").

The semicolon (;) is used to join independent clauses in a sentence when connecting words are omitted. A semicolon is called for when the thoughts in the two independent clauses are close and the writer wishes to emphasize this point or to contrast the two thoughts:

Semicolon for connecting thoughts

Anorexia nervosa is a disorder in which the victims literally starve themselves; despite their emaciated appearance, they consider themselves to be overweight.

In most instances these long sentences can be divided into shorter ones, which may be clearer:

No semicolon

Anorexia nervosa is a disorder in which the victims literally starve themselves. Despite their emaciated appearance, they consider themselves to be overweight.

Use a colon (:) to indicate that a list will follow or to introduce a quotation. The colon essentially tells us "note what follows":

Colon to indicate a list follows

> Subjects were given the following items: (a) four calling birds, (b) three French hens, (c) two turtle doves. . . .

Colon to indicate a quote follows

> Subject B responded: "My feeling about this situation is. . . ."

Double quotation marks (" ") are used to enclose direct quotations, and single quotation marks (' ') indicate a quote within a quote:

Quotation marks

> Subject B responded: "My feeling about this situation was summed up in a nutshell by Jim when he said, 'It's a tough job, but somebody has to do it.' "

Be sure that the appropriate punctuation, whether comma or period, is included *within* the quotation marks; colons and semicolons, however, always come *after* the closing quotation marks. When the quotation chosen is more than four typed or hand-written lines, it is set off from the body of the prose and quotation marks are omitted, as illustrated by the following quotation (which you will recognize from Chapter 2). The quotation begins "As teacher-training institutions . . ." and ends ". . . in the classroom is more her role"; the page numbers on which the quotation appears in Rosenthal and Jacobson's 1968 work are given in parentheses at the end:

Lengthy quotation

> What practical implications do Rosenthal and Jacobson (1968) draw from their research findings? They write:
>
> > As teacher-training institutions begin to teach the possibility that teachers' expectations of their pupils' performance may serve as self-fulfilling prophecies, there may be a new expectancy created. The new expectancy may be that children can learn more than had been believed possible, an expectation held by many educational theorists, though for quite different reasons. . . . The new expectancy, at the very least, will make it more difficult when they encounter the educationally disadvantaged for teachers to think, "Well, after all, what can you expect?" The man on the street may be permitted his opinions and prophecies of the unkempt children loitering in a dreary schoolyard. The teacher in the schoolroom may need to learn that those same prophecies within her may be fulfilled; she is no casual passer-by. Perhaps Pygmalion in the classroom is more her role. (pp. 181–182)

Revising

In the next chapter, we consider the details of assembling your final draft. Revising the first draft of your paper is best done after you have been able to leave the material entirely. When you approach your writing after having taken this break (ideally, of twenty-four hours or more), your own critical powers will be sharp. Syntax errors, lapses in logic, and other problems will become evident, so that smoothing out these sections will be a relatively simple chore.

As you reread, here is a list of "dos" and "don'ts":

- Be concise.
- Break up long paragraphs that contain a lot of disparate ideas into smaller, more coherent paragraphs.
- Be specific.
- Choose words for what they mean, not just for how they sound.
- Double-check punctuation.
- Don't use a long word when a short one will do.
- Don't be redundant ("most unique" or "irregardless").
- Don't let spelling errors mar your writing.

If you are revising your first draft in long hand or with a typewriter, equip yourself with scissors and glue (the retractable stick glue is easiest to use). With these tools, rearranging paragraphs, condensing sentences, and adding or subtracting references will be relatively easy.

Working with a Word Processor

If you are working with a word processor, you know that the steps involved in first drafts, revisions, and final drafts are telescoped. These stages lose their formal definition because the computer allows you, with the stroke of a key, to shift or change words, sentences, paragraphs, even entire sections as you compose. Notes, long quotations, references, tables, and figures can be stored in the computer's memory or on a diskette and retrieved as needed. Word processors also allow you to use an automatic system to monitor your spelling of common English words.

The result is that it is fun to write on the machine. However, the copy that it prints out can be deceptively clean. Do not be captivated by the look of the printed page. Careful scrutiny is still called for, so that your final product is not flawed by errors of omission or lapses in logic.

6

Layout and Typing

With your final draft in hand, we now turn to what is essentially the packaging of your research report or term paper. In this chapter we discuss the specifics involved in the final steps required to produce a finished product.

The First Impression

Study the sample passage at the top of Exhibit 5. If you were the instructor and a student submitted a paper to you that began with this paragraph, what would your first impression be? How many problems did you notice? Did you catch the following typographical errors, omissions, usage errors, and spelling mistakes?

- Typographical error: Pygmaliom
- Spelling mistake: Jacobsen (twice)
- Usage error: phenomena
- Omission: statistically significant
- Spelling mistake: surpased
- Usage error: &
- Typographical error: inthe
- Spelling mistake: intellectule

With a little time and effort the paragraph could have been cleaned up to enhance the student's finished product. Compare the messy paragraph with the carefully edited and cleanly typed paragraph below it to see what a difference a first impression can make.

Helpful Pointers

We assume you will correct spelling mistakes, usage errors, and omissions before you submit your paper. What follows are a few general pointers to consider as you set about the typing of your final draft:

In _Pygmalion in the Classroom_, Rosenthal and
Jacobsen (1968) conclude that the phenomena of the self-
fulfilling prophecy is as viable in the classroom as
Rosenthal and his coworkers previously showed it to be in
the scientist's laboratory. Students whose names were
randomly selected and represented to be "bloomers" showed _statistically significant_
IQ gains that surpased those of students not so labeled for
their teachers. It was the label, Rosenthal & Jacobsen
assert, which created false positive expectations in the
teachers' minds and, in turn, resulted in this difference
in intellectule performance.

In _Pygmalion in the Classroom_, Rosenthal and
Jacobson (1968) conclude that the phenomenon of the self-
fulfilling prophecy is as viable in the classroom as
Rosenthal and his coworkers previously showed it to be in
the scientist's laboratory. Students whose names were
randomly selected and represented to be "bloomers" showed
statistically significant IQ gains that surpassed those of
students not so labeled for their teachers. It was the
label, Rosenthal and Jacobson assert, which created false
positive expectations in the teachers' minds and, in turn,
resulted in this difference in intellectual performance.

Exhibit 5 First impressions count

- Treat yourself to a new typewriter ribbon. It will be frustrating for the
  instructor to have to read a paper with typescript so light or blurry that it
  taxes the eyes.
- Use 8 1/2 x 11-inch white paper, preferably bond. Never use onionskin
  because it tears easily and does not take corrections well. Do not use what is
  commercially called "erasable" paper because it smears readily.
- Double-space the typing on one side of the paper only, numbering pages in
  the upper-right corner.
- Make an extra copy of the paper. The original is for your instructor, and the
  duplicate copy will ensure that there is a spare copy available in case of a
  problem.

- If you are using a word processor and do not have access to a letter-quality printer (daisy wheel printer), use the strikeover mode rather than the first-draft mode to print your final copy.
- If you are using a word processor, let the right margin remain ragged; that is, do not have your program adjust spacing to have all the lines of type of equal length. Use ragged right margins so you do not have trouble with a computer that does not know how to break words correctly.
- Use generous margins. When typing, set your pica typewriter at fifty-five characters per line; for an elite, use sixty-six per line.

We turn now to other specifics of layout and typing that will help to give your paper an inviting look.

Title Page Format

Glance at the title pages in Appendixes A and B. Note that the title of the research report or term paper summarizes the main idea of the project. A good title is succinct and yet adequately descriptive so that it gives the reader the gist of the project at a glance. You probably will have already arrived at a working title when you narrowed your topic. That title can be changed or made more specific if you feel you need to once your project is complete.

The other information shown on the title page of the students' papers is:

- The student's name
- The course or sequence for which the paper was written
- The instructor's name (if submitted for a course) or advisor's name (if submitted to fulfill some other requirement)
- The date the student turned in the paper

Headings

It is customary to break up the text of a manuscript with headings. You can derive these from the outline of your term paper, or in the case of the research report, use the specific headings inherent in the structure of the report (Introduction, Method, and so on). Note how Maria's headings and subheadings lend symmetry to her paper, showing its progressive development in concise phrases:

```
                    Background
Nature of Anorexia Nervosa
Treatment Approaches
                    The Weight Gain Approach
Behavioral Examples
Organic Examples
                    The Weight Gain Plus Therapy Approach
Overview and Examples
```

Conclusions

Summary

Maria's term paper uses two formats of headings: center and flush left. The center heading, used to separate the manuscript into major sections, is written in uppercase and lowercase letters and not underlined. To subdivide the major sections, Maria uses subheadings placed at the left margin (flush left), underlined, and in uppercase and lowercase.

Underlining

Underlining can be used to distinguish levels of headings. Conventional usage also calls for reference works mentioned in the body of the text to be underlined ("In Pygmalion in the Classroom, Rosenthal and Jacobson. . . ."). Underscoring is also used in several other ways:

- Letters used as statistical symbols are underlined: F, N, n, P, p, t, Z, and so on. (Greek letters used as symbols are not underlined, for example, χ^2, Σ, σ.)

- In reference lists, volume numbers of journal articles and titles of books and journals are underlined.

- Works that you wish to emphasize are underscored, but this should be done sparingly ("Effective teaching, the authors imply, will come only from the teachers' firm belief that their pupils can perform. . . .").

Citations in Text

Several simple conventions are recommended by the APA for citation of an author's work in the prose of a paper. Their purpose is to make it easy for the reader to identify the source of a quotation or idea and then to locate the particular reference in the list at the end of the paper. The author-date method of citation is the general format recommended. The surname of the author and the year of publication are inserted in the narrative text at the appropriate point.

Do not list any publication in your reference list that you do not cite. Similarly, do not cite any reference without listing it on the reference list. If you want to cite a source that you did not read, use the following format: "Nelson (1984, as cited by Fung, 1985) observed that. . . ."

In general there are two categories of citations in student research reports and term papers, and you will find examples of each in the sample papers. One category consists of citations that appear as part of the narrative of the paper; the other category consists of citations inserted entirely in parentheses:

Citation appearing as part of narrative

Jaeger, Anthony, and Rosnow (1980) planted a rumor among college students.

Citation entirely in parentheses

> Lithium carbonate has been found to increase the anorectic's intake of fatty foods and thus produce weight gain (Gross, Evert, Goldberg, Faden, Nee, & Kaye, 1980).

These two examples also illustrate some of the conventions of author-date citations. First, the surnames of all the authors are listed (even though in the latter instance this called for six names to be mentioned). It is customary to list all surnames the first time the citation is given, and in subsequent citations to mention only the surname of the first author followed by *et al.* and the date. For example:

Subsequent citation as part of narrative

> This finding is consistent with that of Jaeger et al. (1980) as previously discussed.

Subsequent citation entirely in parentheses

> As mentioned earlier, lithium carbonate was also found to be effective in producing weight gain (Gross et al., 1980).

Second, note that the word *and* was spelled out in the narrative citation but that an ampersand (&) was substituted for *and* in the parenthetical citation. This is also conventional usage the *Publication Manual of the American Psychological Association* recommends.

Other specific rules that cover most simple cases are:

- If you are citing a series of works, the proper sequence is by alphabetical order of the surname of the first author and then by chronological order (Kern, 1960, 1961; Mithalal, 1963, 1964).
- Two works published by the same author in the same year are designated as a, b, c, and so on (1980a, 1980b, 1980c). Alphabetical order of the works' titles determines their sequence.
- Work accepted for publication but not yet printed is designated as "in press" (Bender, in press); in a list of citations the rule is to place this work last (Bender, 1980, 1983, in press).

What should you do if you run into a problem that these rules do not address? If your instructor is a stickler for the APA style of handling citations, then turn to the APA publication manual for more detailed rules and examples. We are not sticklers and only recommend that you keep one general idea in mind as you reach within these specific guidelines—if you run into a problem, use your common sense. Ask yourself whether you could find the one reference referred to based on the citation you provided. In other words, put yourself in the shoes of the reader. For the reader, the citations are like the legend on a map, except that these legends are the key to the reference sources that you list at the end of your paper.

Tables and Figures

As with the title page (and the abstract of the research report), present each table and figure on a separate sheet of paper. Often, when students include tables in their research reports, the instructor finds that they are merely presenting their raw data in a neat format. Save your raw data for the appendix of your report if this is required, and keep in mind that tables in research reports are *summaries* of raw data. The APA rule for articles being submitted for publication is to place tables and figures at the end of the manuscript and to instruct the printer where to place them by typing a note ("Insert Table 1 about here") in the appropriate spot in the body of the narrative. However, since we are talking about student papers and not articles for publication, we recommend a simplified format that we have also found easier to read. As John's research report illustrates, a table or figure is placed on a separate page and inserted just after the one on which it is first introduced in the narrative. To make it easy for the reader to locate, you might write "See page xx" or "As Figure x on the next page shows. . . ."

Note that the title of John's table is shown above the table, whereas the title (or caption) of his figure is indicated beneath the figure. However you choose to display your data, whether in a table or a figure, the title must be clearly and precisely stated. If you need to add some clarifying or explanatory note to your table, it is customary to place this information below the table. For example:

Table note

Note: The possible range of scores was from 1 (strong disagreement) to 5 (strong agreement), with 3 indicating no opinion.

If you want to make specific notes, use superscript lowercase letters (a, b, c) or asterisks (*, **, ***):

Superscript notation

$${}^a\underline{n} = 50 \qquad {}^b\underline{n} = 62$$

Asterisk notation

$$*\underline{p} < .05 \quad **\underline{p} < .01 \quad ***\underline{p} < .005$$

The following specific guidelines may prove helpful as you prepare figures for inclusion in your paper:

- The graphics should be neat, clearly presented, and precisely labeled to augment your discussion.
- For the sake of clarity, the figure should be at least five inches wide.
- It is customary when graphing the relationship between an independent and a dependent variable (or between a predictor variable and a criterion variable) to put the independent (or predictor) variable on the horizontal axis and the dependent (or criterion) variable on the vertical axis. There are exceptions, such as stem-and-leaf plots.
- The units should progress from small to large.
- The data should be precisely plotted. Graph paper can help you keep rows and columns evenly spaced.

It is not necessary to develop elaborate figures and graphs in a student paper. Sometimes elaborate graphics can introduce distortions, thus distracting from a clear, concise summary of the data. If you would like to learn more about how figures and graphs can be inadvertently (or intentionally) misleading, two fascinating works are E. R. Tufte's *The Visual Display of Quantitative Information* (Graphics Press, 1983) and H. Wainer's "How to Display Data Badly" (*The American Statistician*, May 1984).

Reference List

The reference list starts on a new page. The order of references is arranged alphabetically by the surname of the author(s) and then by the date of publication. The APA style is to:

- Invert all authors' names (that is, last name, first name, middle initial). Use commas to separate authors and an ampersand (&) before the last author.
- Give the year the work was copyrighted (the year and month for magazine articles and the year, month, and day for newspaper articles).
- For book titles, capitalize only the first word of the title and of the subtitle, if any, as well as any proper names; for journal titles, capitalize the first word of the title and of the subtitle, if any, and all other words except coordinating conjunctions (*and, or*), articles (*a, an, the*), and prepositions (*in, of, for*).
- Give the issue number of the journal if an article cited is paginated by issue.
- Underline the volume number of a journal article and the title of a book or the name of a journal.
- Give the city of a book's publisher; if the city is not well known or might be confused with another location (for example, Cambridge, Massachusetts, and Cambridge, England), also give the state (or country).

Using these pointers and the following examples as general guidelines, try to be clear, consistent, and complete in listing your source material.

Authored book

Lana, R. E. (1969). Assumptions of social psychology. New York: Appleton-Century-Crofts.

Work in press (technical term capitalized; city and state)

Mullen, B., & Rosenthal, R. (in press). BASIC meta-analysis: Procedures and programs. Hillsdale, NJ: Erlbaum.

Edited work

Gergen, K. J., & Gergen, M. M. (Eds.) (1984). Historical social psychology. Hillsdale, NJ: Erlbaum.

Journal article paginated by volume (three authors)

Arms, R. L., Russell, G. W., & Sandilands, M. L. (1979). Effects on the hostility of spectators viewing aggressive sports. Social Psychology Quarterly, 42, 275–279.

Article paginated by issue

Goldstein, J. H. (1978). In vivo veritas: Has humor research looked at humor? Humor Research Newsletter, 3(1), 3–4.

Article in foreign language (title translated into English)

Foa, U. G. (1966). Le nombre huit dans la socialization de l'enfant [The number eight in the socialization of the infant]. Bulletin du Centre d'Etudes et Recherches Psychologiques, 15, 39–47.

Chapter in multivolume edited series

Kipnis, D. (1984). The use of power in organizations and interpersonal settings. In S. Oskamp (Ed.), Applied social psychology (Vol. 5, pp. 171–210). Beverly Hills, CA: Sage.

Chapter in press in edited book

Blank, T. O. (in press). Contextual and relational perspectives on adult psychology. In R. L. Rosnow & M. Georgoudi (Eds.), Contextualism and understanding in behavioral science: Implications for research and theory. New York: Praeger.

Magazine article

Goldstein, J. H. (1982, August/September). A laugh a day: Can mirth keep disease at bay? The Sciences, pp. 21–25

Technical report

Kipnis, D. M., & Kidder, L. H. (1977). Practice performance and sex: Sex role appropriateness, success and failure as determinants of men's and women's task learning capabilities (Report No. 1). Philadelphia: University City Science Center.

Paper presented at a meeting

Lamberth, J. (1981, January). Jury selection: A psychological approach. Paper presented at the meeting of the American Trial Association, Moorestown, NJ.

Proofing and Correcting

We now come to the final steps before you submit your paper: proofing and correcting. Read the finished manuscript more than once. Ask yourself the following questions:

- Are there omissions?
- Are there misspellings?
- Are the numbers correct?
- Are the hyphenations correct?
- Are all the references cited in the body of your paper in the references section and vice versa? (Personal communications are only cited in the text, as shown in Maria's paper.)

The first time you read your final draft, the appeal of the neat, clean copy can lead you to overlook errors. Try to put the paper aside for twenty-four hours, and then reread it carefully. If you find errors, be sure to correct them before you submit the paper. If they are small mistakes, use correction fluid to cover them and make the required corrections. Do not just type over an incorrect letter or number. It is permissible, however, to insert an inadvertently omitted word. Use a carat (∧) inserted into the line of type, then type or print the omitted word or phrase neatly in the space above the line from which it was omitted. If there is a substantial omission, or a major error to be corrected, retype the entire page.

Give your paper a final look, checking to be sure all the pages are there and in order. Then submit it. If you adhered to the guidelines in this manual, you should have a sense of a job well done and feel confident that the paper will receive the serious attention that a clear, consistent, and attractive manuscript deserves.

Sample Term Paper

Major Treatments for Anorexia Nervosa:
Weight Gain Versus Weight Gain Plus Therapy

Maria Di Medio

Term Paper
Psych 156 Introduction to Abnormal Psychology
Cabrini College
(Date Submitted)

Background

Nature of Anorexia Nervosa

Anorexia nervosa is the technical term for a disorder occurring mostly among adolescent females, although it has been known to occur in males and in patients in other age brackets. A constellation of symptoms could include loss of at least 25 percent of original weight, a distorted body image, cessation or delay of the menstrual period (amenorrhea) in women, and hair loss.

In this paper I shall concentrate on the treatment of anorexia nervosa. The victims of this illness literally starve themselves. This results in dramatic weight losses and can even lead to death. However, in spite of their emaciated appearance, they perceive themselves as layered in fat, a condition that they abhor and try desperately to change.

Treatment Approaches

There are two major treatment approaches to be discussed in this paper. One approach involves focusing on the weight loss as the symptom to be treated. Within this category of treatment there are the operant conditioning procedure and the desensitization procedure, which collectively are termed the behavioral approaches to weight gain. Also falling into this category are organic procedures, characterized by the administration of drugs and force-feeding (hyperalimentation).

The other principal approach that I shall discuss focuses on the weight loss along with the victim's psychological problems as the symptoms to be treated. Variations of psychotherapy in combination with behavioral or organic procedures of weight gain illustrate this approach. Family therapy is one such psychotherapeutic variation, which focuses on psychological problems emanating from the family's relationship with the anorectic.

The Weight Gain Approach

Behavioral Examples

A case dealing with a 37-year-old anorectic woman exemplifies the operant conditioning approach to weight gain (Bachrach, Erwin, & Mohr, 1965). This woman weighed only 47 pounds when the treatment was begun. At first, she was deprived of any positive reinforcements, such as music and visitors. She then ate her meals in the presence of either a psychologist, a medical student, or a resident and was given verbal reinforcements when she made efforts to eat. Eventually, weight gain was the criterion upon which she received reinforcers. On her release from the hospital, the patient's family continued reinforcing her efforts and helped maintain her eating behavior. By the end of the program, the patient had increased her weight to 88 pounds.

However, in a follow-up study, Erwin (1977) states that this patient then dropped down to 55 pounds 14 years later. This might have been a result of the patient's eating inadequate amounts of food, even though she apparently continued her regimen of eating on schedule. The patient showed improvement in her social life, becoming involved in a number of activities. Despite her precarious weight, she seemed to become more self-sufficient. In another study, the effects of operant conditioning have been found to differ little between hospital patients receiving behavior modification and those who did not undergo behavior modification (Eckert, Goldberg, Halmi, Casper, & Davis, 1979).

Systematic desensitization in treating anorexia nervosa focuses on the anxiety associated with eating. In one study, desensitization was used with a 23-year-old woman who had rapidly lost 20 pounds and displayed anxiety about eating (Lang, 1965). She often did not eat when she was in new surroundings or at odds with someone. Hierarchies were established for specific fear-eliciting stimuli: traveling, disapproval, and being the center of attention. During desensitization she was offered candy. Although she was desensitized in these areas, her eating problem could not be effectively remediated. However, it is questionable whether the subject had been properly diagnosed as having anorexia. Her refusal to eat may have been a reaction to stressful situations rather than an obsessive preoccupation with not eating. Another reason to question the presence of anorexia is that the subject did not seem to exhibit the distortion in body perception commonly found in anorectics.

Behavioral procedures for treating anorexia nervosa seem to have their shortcomings when used alone. Bruch (1979) claimed that the weight gain achieved by behavior modification techniques is rather short lived, since the underlying psychological problems associated with the illness are ignored. Depriving anorectics of their privileges has also been problematic (Bemis, 1978). Nevertheless, an evaluation of the efficacy of behavior therapy has been difficult due to a lack of follow-up studies (Bemis, 1978) and the small numbers of patients used in the studies. The administration of medications simultaneously with the behavioral treatment (Eckert et al., 1979) has further confounded attempts to evaluate this mode of treatment.

Organic Examples

Organic procedures to achieve weight gain have included tube feeding (hyperalimentation) and the administration of drugs. Lithium carbonate has been found to increase the anorectic's intake of fatty foods and thus produce weight gain (Gross, Evert, Goldberg, Faden, Nee, & Kay, 1980). Although it is not known how this drug directly affects weight, it may have an effect on glucose metabolism and thereby cause a desire to eat. Lithium carbonate also seems to affect anorectics' perception of their illness. Those treated with this drug did not deny their illness as much as those who did not receive the drug. In spite of such reports, organic approaches have also been criticized since they do not take into account patients' psychological status but only their weight loss problem (Andersen, 1979; Bemis, 1978).

The Weight Gain Plus Therapy Approach

Overview and Examples

   In this mode of treatment, a weight gain regimen is established and is accompanied by, or followed by, psychotherapy. In therapy the patient's problems are worked out; family members may also seek counseling regarding the anorectic as well as themselves. One general view underlying the psychotherapeutic approach is that the victims are seen as perfectionists who strive to please the real or imagined standards of their family. Another view is that patients' behavior is an attempt to manipulate their families in order to gain control over their own lives. Various combinations of weight gain treatments with therapy have been tried (Geller, 1975; Maloney & Farrell, 1980).

   One study reported success with a behavioral method of individual therapy (Geller, 1975). A 22-year-old female not only gained weight but also felt more in control of her body after therapy. She was capable of expressing her feelings about eating more openly. However, long term results are needed. Hyperalimentation with therapy has led to improvement in terms of weight gain, social behavior, concentration, and expression of feelings (Maloney & Farrell, 1980).

   Bruch (1979) has recommended that satisfactory weight gain be achieved before starting therapy. She suggests that therapy should begin when the anorectic weighs around 90 to 95 pounds. She underscores the importance of getting rid of maladaptive distortions about eating prior to working out the patient's other problems. Bruch's use of therapy on an anorectic male showed that once the anorectic understood what he was doing to his body, he was able to feel in control not only of his body but of his life in general.

   In a number of programs, an integrated approach to weight gain is used in treating the individual. One such program (Lucas, Duncan, & Piens, 1976) consisted of (a) separating anorectics from their familes, (b) establishing a weight gain approach involving eating under supervision and eventually having patients eat by themselves, (c) psychotherapy involving a physiatrist to help the patient maintain weight and a therapist to treat distorted perception, and (d) family counseling or therapy for other members. This program was effective in improving anorectics' relationship with their families and friends and in alleviating the depression and listlessness patients had experienced.

In another example (A. Andersen, personal communication, November 10, 1980), the integrated approach started with (a) nutritional restitution, then (b) individual therapy when the patient was at 90 to 95 percent of ideal weight, along with group and family therapy, next (c) placing reponsibilities of eating (among other activities) onto the patient, and finally (d) a follow-up to see whether the patient readapted to his or her former environment without relapse. Although Andersen (1979) claims that this is perhaps the best approach in treating anorectics, approximately 50 percent improved with some symptoms remaining (e.g., preoccupation with food) while 25 percent remained very ill.

Family Therapy

Family therapy for the anorectic directly involves the family in helping the patient to adjust. The disorder is viewed as a family problem involving the patient's role in the family and the attitudes of family members toward the disorder (Minuchin, Rosman, & Baker, 1978). An anorectic in an inpatient program usually undergoes behavior modification to change eating patterns. The family first meets with professionals and then all have a luncheon session, which also includes the anorectic. This session is structured so that the family can badger the anorectic about the eating problem or it can overlook the problem. The anorectic usually starts eating after the luncheon session. Out of 53 patients, 86 percent were effectively treated by family therapy. The highest cure rate was among younger anorectics, who had experienced the disorder for a briefer period. To be sure, some families are reluctant to venture into this mode of treatment, perhaps for fear of worsening the situation with the revelation of problems long buried or for fear of being found to be at fault themselves.

Conclusions

In a comparison of treatments focusing solely on weight gain with those incorporating weight gain plus therapy, there seems to be an indication that the latter approach is more effective in treating anorexia nervosa. This can be attributed to the attention given to patients' psychological problems underlying their disorder. The weight gain method may affect eating habits, but its efficacy is short lived if the patient's distorted perceptions about eating and other personal conflicts are not treated. Therefore, weight gain with therapy should indicate a higher cure rate for anorectics. However, more longitudinal studies are needed to determine the most effective mode of treatment for all anorectics.

Summary

Two major treatment approaches to anorexia nervosa were discussed. In one type the focus was on weight gain, and in the other type the focus was on weight gain as well as the patient's underlying psychological disorder(s). Several examples of each type were described, and the conclusion drawn was that the combinatory approach was more effective. Background sources for this discussion included recent literature on anorexia nervosa and information obtained from correspondence with professionals.

References

Andersen, A. (1979). Anorexia nervosa: Diagnosis and treatment. Weekly Psychiatry Update Series (Report No. 3). Princeton, NJ: Biomedia Inc.

Bachrach, A., Erwin, W., & Mohr, J. (1965). The control of eating behavior in an anorectic by operant conditioning techniques. In L. P. Ullman & L. Krasner (Eds.), Case studies in behavior modification. New York: Holt, Rinehart & Winston.

Bemis, K. (1978). Current approaches to the etiology and treatment of anorexia nervosa. Psychological Bulletin, 85, 593-617.

Bruch, H. (1979). The golden cage: The enigma of anorexia nervosa. New York: Vintage Books.

Eckert, E., Goldberg, S., Halmi, K., Casper, R., & Davis, J. (1979). Behavior therapy in anorexia nervosa. British Journal of Psychiatry, 134, 55-59.

Erwin, W. (1977). A 16 yrs. follow up case of severe anorexia nervosa. Journal of Behavior and Experimental Psychiatry, 84, 157-160.

Geller, J. (1975). Treatment of anorexia nervosa by the integration of behavior therapy and psychotherapy. Psychotherapy and Psychosomatics, 26, 167-177.

Gross, H., Evert, M., Goldberg, S., Faden, V., Nee, L., & Kaye, W. (1980). A double blind controlled trial of lithium carbonate in primary anorexia nervosa. Unpublished manuscript, NIMH Clinical Center, Bethesda, MD.

Lang, P. (1965). Behavior therapy with a case of nervous anorexia. In L. Ullman & L. Krasner (Eds.), Case studies in behavior modification. New York: Holt, Rinehart & Winston.

Lucas, A., Duncan, J., & Piens, V. (1976). The treatment of anorexia nervosa. American Journal of Psychiatry, 133, 1034-1038.

Maloney, M., & Farrell, M. (1980). Treatment of severe weight
    loss in anorexia nervosa with hyperalimentation and
    psychotherapy. <u>American Journal of Psychiatry,</u> <u>137,</u> 314-318.
Minuchin, S., Rosman, B., & Baker, L. (1978). <u>Psychosomatic</u>
    <u>families: Anorexia nervosa in context</u>. Cambridge, MA:
    Harvard University Press.

Sample Research Report

Confidence in Rumor and the Likelihood of Transmission:
A Correlational Study

John H. Yost

Research Report
Temple University Honors Sequence
Advisor: Prof. R. L. Rosnow
(Date Submitted)

Abstract

The question as to whether individuals are more likely to transmit rumors when they are confident in the truth of the rumor was addressed during tense labor negotiations. The participants were faculty members of a university that was in the midst of labor negotiations between the faculty union and the university administration. Participants were asked to complete a questionnaire in which they reported any rumors that they had heard concerning the ongoing negotiations, whether or not they had transmitted the rumors, and their confidence in the truth of the rumors. As hypothesized, there was a positive linear relationship between confidence in the truth of a rumor and the likelihood of its transmission.

Introduction

Rumor is defined as a proposition for belief that is unverified and in general circulation. A current rumor theory (Rosnow, 1980) identifies internal variables as being essential to the amount of rumor in circulation (i.e., rumor strength). The amount of rumor in circulation is asserted to be a complex function of anxiety (an emotional factor) and uncertainty (a cognitive factor). These two conditions, when stimulated by ongoing events, are posited to be linearly related to rumor strength. Therefore, when a situation elicits little anxiety or uncertainty, the low levels of arousal generate no rumors. At the other extreme, when a situation elicits high levels of anxiety and uncertainty, there is a more urgent desire to reduce the emotional and cognitive states. In other words, the greater the anxiety and uncertainty, the greater is the need to alleviate the discomfort.

Knapp (1944) observed that rumors thrive in periods of social stress. Current rumor theory is consistent with this observation, and different investigations of rumor concern periods of obvious discomfort, such as a catastrophe or a war (Allport & Lepkin, 1945; Knapp, 1944; Nkpa, 1975; Prasad, 1935), but none have actually collected data on the rate of rumor transmission. Data concerning why individuals transmit certain rumors they hear and not others would be valuable in helping us to understand the phenomenon of rumor.

Why is it that some rumors are transmitted with greater alacrity than others during stressful situations? In this study it was hypothesized that the more confidence one has in the truth of a rumor, the more likely one is to transmit the rumor. This hypothesis proceeds on the idea that one's credibility is at stake when a rumor is transmitted. It should be to one's advantage to pass information that has a good chance of being true rather than information that is likely to prove false. Passing false rumors could jeopardize one's future credibility, while passing rumors that prove true could enhance one's future credibility.

There is already some experimental evidence that supports the idea of a relationship between confidence in rumor and rumor transmission. Jaeger, Anthony, and Rosnow (1980) planted a rumor among college students. In one condition the rumor was refuted by a confederate, and in another condition the rumor was not refuted. Subjects in the refutation groups reported lower initial belief in the rumor than subjects in the nonrefutation groups, and the rumor was circulated with lower frequency when refuted. The present study sought to determine whether this relationship found in an experimental setting with college students also held true in a field setting with another population of subjects. The question addressed was whether there was a relationship between confidence in the truth of rumors and rumor transmission during a period of stressful labor negotiations.

Method

In this study, rumors were collected during a stressful period of time. A university community was divided over contract negotiations between the faculty union and the university administration. The faculty union had voted to strike if a contract agreement were not reached by a specific date. Publicly, the administration refused to negotiate on the faculty union's major demand. The university community was gripped with tension as the strike deadline approached. There was much speculation as to whether or not there would be a strike, as well as what to do should a strike occur. The data in this study were collected in the week prior to the strike deadline, when tensions were high. Only a last-minute settlement averted a strike, and most members of the university community were unclear about the situation until the final moments.

Questionnaires were placed in the interoffice mailboxes of 505 full-time faculty members from 28 different departments one morning, 10 days before the strike deadline. The instructions asked the recipients to list any rumors that they had heard over the past several days that pertained to the ongoing labor negotiations at the university. Rumor was defined as "any report, statement, or story that one may have heard or mentioned for which there is no immediate evidence available to verify its truth." After reporting each rumor, the respondents were asked to indicate whether or not the rumor was transmitted and to rate their confidence in the truth of the rumor on a 0 to 10 scale. Zero represented "no confidence in the truth of the rumor," and 10 represented "strong confidence in the truth of the rumor." The anonymity of the respondents' answers was ensured, and they were asked to return the completed questionnaire through the interoffice mail within 7 days (3 days before the strike deadline). There were 55 questionnaires returned, for a response rate of 11 percent.

Results

In those 55 questionnaires there were 134 responses purported to be "rumors" by the respondents. These 134 items were classified by two independent raters as positive rumors, negative rumors, or nonrumors. There were 20 items that were classified as nonrumors, leaving a total of 114 rumors.

Rumors were classified as "positive" if the judges inferred that the outcome of the rumor would be beneficial to the respondent. Examples of such rumors included the following:

--Even if there were to be a strike, the faculty would not
   lose any pay.

--The administration is ready to settle.

Rumors were classified as "negative" if the judges inferred that the outcome of the rumor would be detrimental to the respondent. Examples of such rumors were:

--The administration wants a strike to break the union.

--All faculty benefits will be stopped if a strike occurs;
   this is in addition to stopping salaries.

Of the 114 rumors reported, 22 were classified as positive and 92 as negative. Within both positive and negative categories, the confidence ratings were collapsed to form three levels of confidence--low (ratings of 0 to 3), moderate (4 to

6), and high (7 to 10). The results are shown in Table 1 (see page 7) in terms of the percentages of positive and negative rumors reported as having been transmitted at each of the three levels of confidence--and again in Figure 1 (see page 8). A linear trend analysis, employing a contrast analytic procedure described by Rosenthal and Rosnow (1984, 1985), was used to analyze the data.

As Figure 1 clearly shows, there was an increasing linear relationship between confidence in rumor and transmission rate. For negative rumors, the Z of significance of the linear contrast was highly significant (Z = 5.670, p < .00003 one-tail). The effect size was also impressive, with r = .591. For positive rumors, the results were more conservative but impressive nonetheless, Z = 2.002, p = .02 one-tail, r = .427. While these results do not prove causality, they are nevertheless consistent with the idea that individuals are more inclined to pass rumors they believe than rumors they do not believe.

Discussion

This research finding is consistent with current rumor theory, which asserts that when a situation elicits high anxiety and uncertainty, there is a more urgent desire to reduce the emotional and cognitive discomfort. This desire to alleviate discomfort will often result in rumor transmission where individuals try to make sense of a situation and to assess possible future outcomes. If someone has low confidence in the truth of a rumor, upon transmission this person's anxiety and uncertainty may not decrease--it may even increase because of the added stress of transmitting information that may be false and potentially damaging to one's credibility. Therefore, individuals may have a tendency not to pass a rumor when they do not have much confidence in its veracity. On the other hand, the more confidence people have in the truth of a rumor, the more effective will be the alleviation of discomfort as they transmit

Table 1

Rates of Transmission of Rumors

Level of Confidence	Negative Rumors (percent)	Positive Rumors (percent)
High	86.1	71.4
Moderate	52.4	42.9
Low	31.4	25.0

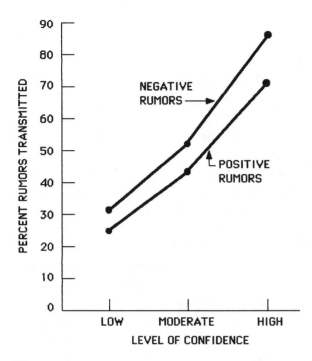

Figure 1 Transmission rate as a function of low, moderate, and high confidence in truth of negative and positive rumors

the rumor. Even if it serves only to verify a problem, the rumor provides a basis for making plans to confront the troubling situation.

In other words, for positive rumors, the alleviation of discomfort may be a reinforcement of an expected outcome of a rumor. The uneasiness of "getting one's hopes up only to be later disappointed" is alleviated. For example, if a faculty member hears that the strike will not occur and has confidence in the truth of the rumor, since it is a stressful situation the individual may transmit the rumor to find support for the belief—which will alleviate discomfort because the expectation of a strike occurring has been minimized by reassuring feedback from others. For negative rumors, the alleviation of discomfort may come in the form of a plan to cope with the ramifications of the outcome of the rumor. For example, if an individual has confidence in a rumor stating that there is going to be a strike, the person may transmit the rumor in order to assess what to do in case of a strike.

Another possible alleviation of discomfort that comes from transmitting rumors that you have confidence in is to have social sanction to say negative things about others (Knapp, 1944). For example, 25 percent of all negative rumors in this study (20 percent of all rumors) were hostile, i.e., assigning the blame for an imminent strike to the president of the university or the administration. This is analogous to a worker who dislikes a manager saying hostile things about the manager via rumors, which is a normatively acceptable form of disparagement during a stressful situation. In this way, rumors may have a purging effect.

Further investigation is warranted to see if the findings of the study are generalizable across other naturalistic settings. With reports of rumors continuing to proliferate recently—for example, in the stock market (Wiggins, 1985) and the business world (Esposito & Rosnow, 1983)—additional research on the topic is needed.

References

Allport, F. H., & Lepkin, M. (1945). Wartime rumors of waste and special privilege: Why some people believe them. _Journal of Abnormal and Social Psychology, 40_, 3-36.

Esposito, J. L., & Rosnow, R. L. (1983). Corporate rumors: How they start and how to stop them. _Management Review, 72_(4), 44-49.

Jaeger, M. E., Anthony, S., & Rosnow, R. L. (1980). Who hears what from whom and with what effect: A study of rumor. _Personality and Social Psychology Bulletin, 6_, 473-478.

Knapp, R. H. (1944). A psychology of rumor. _Public Opinion Quarterly, 8_, 22-37.

Nkpa, N.K.U. (1975). Rumormongering in war time. _Public Opinion Quarterly, 96_, 27-35.

Prasad, J. (1935). The psychology of rumor: A study relating to the great Indian earthquake of 1934. _British Journal of Psychology, 26_, 1-15.

Rosenthal, R., & Rosnow, R. L. (1984). _Essentials of behavioral research: Methods and data analysis_. New York: McGraw-Hill.

Rosenthal, R., & Rosnow, R. L. (1985). _Contrast analysis: Focused comparisons in the analysis of variance_. Cambridge, England: Cambridge University Press.

Rosnow, R. L. (1980). Psychology of rumor reconsidered. _Psychological Bulletin, 87_, 578-591.

Wiggins, P. H. (1985, Feb. 14). Safeway rise and rumors. _The New York Times_.

Appendix: Statistical Computations

Negative Rumors

	low	mod.	high
yes	11	11	31
no	24	10	5
$\sum$	35	21	36

	low	mod.	high
P	.31	.52	.86
S_p^2	.0061	.0119	.0033
λ	-1	0	$+1$

$$Z = \frac{.31(-1) + .52(0) + .86(+1)}{\sqrt{.0061(1) + .0119(0) + .0033(1)}}$$

$$= \boxed{5.6701}$$

$$r = \frac{5.6701}{\sqrt{92}} = \boxed{.5911}$$

Positive Rumors

	low	mod.	high
yes	2	3	5
no	6	4	2
$\sum$	8	7	7

	low	mod.	high
P	.25	.43	.71
S_p^2	.0234	.0350	.0294
λ	-1	0	$+1$

$$Z = \frac{.25(-1) + .43(0) + .71(+1)}{\sqrt{.0234(1) + .0350(0) + .0294(1)}}$$

$$= \boxed{2.0017}$$

$$r = \frac{2.0017}{\sqrt{22}} = \boxed{.4268}$$

Index